F O U R T H   E D I T I O N

stuttering: an integration of contemporary therapies

BARRY GUITAR

THEODORE J. PETERS

THE
STUTTERING
FOUNDATION®

PUBLICATION NO. 0016

stuttering: an integration of contemporary therapies

Publication No. 16

Third Edition—2003
Fourth Edition—2007
2nd Printing—2008

Published by

Stuttering Foundation of America
P.O. Box 11749
Memphis, Tennessee 38111-0749

Library of Congress Catalog Card Number: 99-70789
ISBN 0-933388-41-1

To the Reader

This book grew out of a conference the Stuttering Foundation held in 1978 when an integration of contemporary therapies was far more controversial than it is today.

The authors of this book show how it is possible and desirable to integrate and coordinate the two most commonly used therapy approaches and retain the advantages of both methods in order to obtain even more satisfactory results.

We believe that after reading this book you will feel that the authors deserve a lot of credit for this clear explanation of how to integrate stuttering treatment procedures.

Jane Fraser
President

The Stuttering Foundation

Original Conference Panel—1978

Table of Contents

Introduction

Since 1956 when the Stuttering Foundation of America held its first conference, it has been committed to developing materials for students and practicing clinicians to help them provide the best possible therapy for people who stutter. These materials include books on the prevention of stuttering, treatment of stuttering in children, adolescents, and adults.

Most of these earlier books advocate an approach to stuttering that is referred to in this current book as **stuttering modification** therapy, which will be defined in the following chapter. This book introduces another strategy, focused on increasing fluency in people who stutter rather than having them modify their stuttering. This approach, which will be referred to as **fluency shaping** therapy in this book, will be defined and extensively discussed in the following chapter.

During the 1970's and 1980's there was considerable controversy between the proponents of these two major approaches to the treatment of stuttering. In recent years, however, many clinicians have found that these two approaches are not necessarily antagonistic. On the contrary, techniques based upon one approach can be helpful to the clinician employing the other approach.

The goal of this book is to integrate a stuttering modification approach with a fluency shaping approach. It is hoped that this publication will help to resolve some of the conflicts and mis-understandings that remain in the field today. In writing this book the authors had in mind the student who is studying to become a speech-language pathologist, as well as the practicing clinician, both of whom are confronted with conflicting views as to how to treat the problem of stuttering.

We hope we can help them resolve the controversies.[1] The authors assume the reader is familiar with the procedures of both approaches. The reader who is not familiar with these procedures may wish to read *Therapy for Stutterers* (1974), *Nature & Treatment of Stuttering* (Curlee & Siegel,1997), and *Stuttering and Related Disorders of Fluency* (Conture & Curlee, 2007) and other references cited in this book.

It should be pointed out that the definitions, opinions, and suggestions stated in this book are based upon the authors' training and clinical experience and that they are responsible for them. Both authors were initially trained in stuttering modification therapy and used this type of therapy early in their careers. Later in their careers, however, both authors became familiar with and used fluency shaping therapy and have integrated stuttering modification therapy and fluency shaping therapy in their work.

---

[1] For a further discussion of these issues, the reader may wish to see Controversies about Stuttering Therapy (Gregory, 1979) and Stuttering and Related Disorders of Fluency (Curlee, 1999), especially Chapter 15, "Principles and Practices of Current Stuttering Therapy."

Chapter 1

comparison of stuttering modification and fluency shaping therapies

Definitions

Stuttering Modification Therapy

In this book stuttering modification therapy refers to an approach based on the theory that most of the stutterer's problems in speaking are the result of avoiding or struggling with disfluencies (repetitions, prolongations, and/or blocks), avoiding feared words, and/or avoiding feared situations. The process of therapy includes reducing avoidance behaviors, speech related fears, and negative attitudes toward speech. Very importantly, it also includes helping the client learn to modify the form of his stuttering.[1]

This can be done in a variety of ways. For example, a client can reduce his struggle behavior and smooth out the form of his stuttering. He can also reduce the tension and rapidity of his stuttering to stutter in a more relaxed and deliberate manner. The reader is referred to Van Riper (1973), Williams (1971), Manning (1996), Shapiro (1999), Conture (2001) and previous Stuttering Foundation of America publications (1974, 1978, 2004) for discussions of stuttering modification approaches to treatment.

---

[1] In this book we will use the masculine pronoun when referring to stuttering clients and female pronouns for speech-language pathologists.

Fluency Shaping Therapy

Fluency shaping therapy is based on operant conditioning and programming principles, e.g., successive approximations of a target response, use of reinforcement of appropriate responses, and so on. In a fluency shaping therapy program, some form of fluency is first established in a controlled stimulus situation. This fluency is reinforced and gradually modified to approximate normal conversational speech in the clinical setting. This speech is then generalized to the person's daily speaking environment. For a description of several representative fluency shaping therapy programs the reader is referred to *Conditioning in Stuttering Therapy* (1970), Curlee & Siegel (1997), and Conture & Curlee (2007).

Basic Similarities and Differences

Stuttering modification therapy and fluency shaping therapy can be compared in many ways. We feel, however, that the following six comparisons are the most important with regard to the treatment of stuttering. Four of these comparisons pertain to the goals of therapy, and two are concerned with clinical procedures. The four goal comparisons relate to

1) feelings and attitudes,

2) speech behaviors,

3) fluency maintaining strategies, and

4) general communication skills.

The two clinical procedure comparisons deal with: 1) structure of therapy and 2) data collection. First, we will compare the two therapy approaches with regard to their goals.

Feelings and Attitudes

Stuttering modification therapy places a great deal of emphasis upon reducing the fear of stuttering. Much of the therapy is concerned with reducing the fear of stuttering and eliminating the avoidance behavior associated with this fear. Stuttering modification therapy adherents are also interested in developing positive attitudes toward speaking.

2

They encourage the stutterer to develop an approach attitude toward speaking situations, rather than an avoidance attitude. Stutterers are encouraged to seek out speaking situations that they formerly avoided.

Finally, many stuttering modification therapy clinicians are concerned with improving the stutterer's overall adjustment. They attempt to improve the stutterer's social and vocational skills within the limits of their clinical abilities.

Fluency shaping therapy clinicians do not directly attempt to reduce the stutterer's fear and avoidance of words and speaking situations. This is not one of their stated goals. We feel, however, that often their programming leads to a reduction in fear.

Further, fluency shaping therapy clinicians usually do not make direct attempts to improve the client's attitudes. Again, however, we feel that often the client develops a positive attitude toward speaking as a by-product of this therapy. Through generalization of fluency to previously feared speaking situations, fears and avoidances associated with these situations are often reduced.

Finally, fluency shaping therapy clinicians usually do not make direct attempts to improve the stutterer's social or vocational adjustment, though again this may happen as a by-product of therapy.

Speech Behaviors

Before we outline the speech behavior goals of each approach, we first need to define some terms we will be using. These terms are **spontaneous fluency, controlled fluency,** and **acceptable stuttering.**

By spontaneous fluency we mean a normal level of speech flow that contains neither tension nor struggle behaviors, nor does it contain more than an occasional number of repetitions and prolongations. This fluency is not maintained by paying attention to speech or by changing speaking rate; rather, the person just talks and pays attention to his ideas. It is the fluency of the normal speaker.

3

Controlled fluency is similar to spontaneous fluency except that the speaker must attend to his manner of speaking to maintain relatively normal sounding fluency. He may do this by monitoring the auditory and/or proprioceptive feedback of his speech. He may monitor his speech rate, or he may use preparatory sets and pull-outs to maintain his fluency. Whether he uses these or other techniques, the speaker exhibits normal sounding speech by paying attention to how he is talking.

Finally, acceptable stuttering refers to a level of speech flow where the speaker exhibits noticeable but not severe disfluency and feels comfortable speaking despite his disfluency. As with controlled fluency, the stutterer may be attending to his manner of speaking to maintain this acceptable level of stuttering.

Now, with these definitions in mind, we can discuss the speech behavior goals held by each of the two approaches. We believe that the stuttering modification therapy advocates see their ultimate goal for the stutterer to be spontaneous fluency.

If this is unobtainable, then for some stuttering modification clinicians controlled fluency would be the next goal. For these clinicians, if a stutterer is unable to obtain this controlled fluency, then acceptable stuttering would become the goal. Other stuttering modification clinicians, however, do not advocate controlled fluency; rather, they advocate acceptable stuttering when spontaneous fluency cannot be achieved.

We believe that the adherents of fluency shaping therapy also have as their ultimate goal the attainment of spontaneous fluency. If this is not possible, then controlled fluency would become their goal, along with naturalness of speech. Acceptable stuttering, however, would not be a goal for many fluency shaping therapy adherents. This would be regarded as a program failure.

Both stuttering modification and fluency shaping approaches attempt to achieve spontaneous fluency or controlled fluency, helping the stutterer become more fluent by teaching him to talk, at least temporarily, in a modified, controlled, or purposeful fashion. The methods used to achieve spontaneous or controlled fluency, however, differ somewhat for the two approaches.

Stuttering modification therapy reduces fears and avoidances as one means of enhancing fluency. The stutterer is then taught that he can talk more fluently if he uses certain techniques to modify his stuttering.

Fluency shaping therapy, on the other hand, usually focuses on speech behavior alone, not fears and avoidances. This approach is characterized by establishing stutter-free speech in a controlled speaking situation. It is the overall manner of speaking rather than the moment of stuttering that is modified.

We have observed that these two approaches may produce speech patterns that often sound similar. As clients in each therapy become more spontaneously fluent, they pass through a stage of controlled fluency in which words are spoken with a prolonged, gradual onset. The pull-outs and preparatory sets of stuttering modification therapy may be indistinguishable from the gentle onsets or smooth speech patterns of some fluency shaping therapies.

Fluency Maintaining Strategies

Stuttering modification and fluency shaping approaches employ different techniques to help the stutterer maintain his fluency. Stuttering modification clinicians urge their clients not to avoid words or situations. They stress the importance of nonavoiding and keeping speech fears at a minimum level. Stuttering modification clinicians also teach their clients strategies or techniques to cope with feared words. They teach the stutterer how to approach feared words or how to work through words on which they have already begun to stutter.

Many stuttering modification clinicians also try to foster maintenance of fluency by enhancing the client's social and emotional adjustment. These clinicians will counsel the stutterer in particular problem areas and may refer him to another professional if problems are serious. The stutterer's morale and self-esteem are seen as important considerations for fluency maintenance.

Fluency shaping clinicians, on the other hand, do not generally deal with the stutterer's fears, attitudes, or general adjustment. Rather, they stress maintenance of fluency by such techniques as slowing speech rate, monitoring speech carefully, or paying particular attention to the easy onset of speech. In fluency shaping programs the client is also expected to be as fluent as he possibly can in a given stimulus situation.

If the above techniques break down, the stutterer is expected to use programming principles in addition to the above techniques to reinstate his fluency. For example, if a stutterer generalizes his fluency to his employment setting, but then relapses, he is expected to practice fluency in easier speaking situations, gradually proceeding through successively more difficult situations until he has re-established fluency at work. In other words, in fluency shaping therapy, maintenance procedures consist essentially of having the stutterer recycle himself through the same steps that he went through in his original therapy.

The fluency shaping clinician may also explore environmental contingencies for stuttering. Some stutterers may be living or working in environments which have rewarded their stuttering in the past and which continue to do so after treatment. One example is the spouse who does most of the speaking for the person who stutters. In such cases, environmental contingencies for stuttering and fluency must be rearranged, through mutual planning, to reinforce fluency rather than stuttering.

General Communication Skills

Before we discuss the goals of each approach with regard to communication skills, it might be best to discuss what we have in mind in this area. We mean a variety of things.

First of all, many people who stutter also have other speech and language disorders. In some cases children are referred for stuttering and upon evaluation are found to have delayed speech and/or language development in addition to their stuttering. In other cases, a child referred for an articulation or language disorder may become markedly disfluent while in therapy. Most experienced speech-language pathologists have encountered children like these.

A second consideration under the heading of general communication skills is the enhancement of speech flow. Some clinicians recommend that stutterers in therapy need to work on such aspects of speech as phrasing, pausing, intonation patterns or organization of their verbal output in addition to fluency.

Finally, and less obvious, however, are communication problems that remain or are sometimes created after the stutterer becomes more fluent as a result of therapy. We have seen stutterers who have become quite fluent following therapy, but who still lack conversational skills.

A typical example would be the young man who is no longer afraid to talk to a young woman, but who doesn't know what to say when he meets one. Another example we have seen is the stutterer who, fluent for the first time in his life, begins to monopolize conversations. This is like a child with a new toy who will not give anyone else a chance to play with it. In some cases these now fluent stutterers carry this behavior to such an extreme that they begin to irritate their listeners. These stutterers need training in conversational skills. These are the types of considerations we have in mind when we talk about communication skills in this section.

We believe that neither the stuttering modification nor the fluency shaping approach has addressed itself to these areas of communication skills sufficiently. Stuttering modification therapy has given only minimal consideration to one of these areas: enhancement of speech flow after stuttering behavior is reduced. A number of stuttering modification clinicians suggest that the stutterer should work on a smooth flow of verbal output after moments of stuttering have been reduced or eliminated. Interpersonal communication is not addressed.

Some fluency shaping clinicians also suggest that organization and flow of verbal output may be an important consideration for treatment. As far as we can tell, advocates of fluency shaping have written only minimally about other aspects of general communication skills.

Some description of enhancement of communication skills in stuttering therapy is provided by Craig, A., Hancock, K., Chang, E., McCready, C., Shepley, A., McCaul, A., Costello, D., Harding, S., Kehren, R., Masel, C., & Reilly, K. (1996). A controlled clinical trial for stuttering in persons aged 9 to 14 years. *Journal of Speech and Hearing Research,* 39, 808-826, Neilson (1999) and Rustin, Cook, and Spence (1995). However, it is our belief that communication problems in a general sense should receive more consideration by clinicians working in either framework with stutterers of all ages.

Structure of Therapy

Stuttering modification therapy is usually conducted within a teaching/counseling situation. The stutterer and the clinician typically interact in a loosely structured manner. Fluency shaping therapy, on the other hand, is usually performed in a highly structured situation. Specific instructions and materials are prescribed. Specific responses are called for from the stutterer with specific reactions to these responses required from the clinician. In summary, the two approaches differ substantially with regard to the use of programming principles in structuring therapy.

Data Collection

Traditionally, stuttering modification clinicians do not put a great deal of emphasis upon the collecting and reporting of objective data, e.g., the frequency of stuttering before and after therapy. Stuttering modification clinicians tend to regard as more valid their and the client's descriptions and impressions of the client's stuttering. Fluency shaping clinicians, on the other hand, with their roots in behavior modification, put a great deal of emphasis upon the collection and reporting of objective and reliable data. Both approaches are beginning to seek ways to assess the outcome of therapy, in line with an evidence-based practice approach to stuttering treatment.

Summarizing this section, stuttering modification and fluency shaping therapies are similar in some important ways and different in others. With regard to therapy goals, stuttering modification therapy emphasizes the reduction of speech fears and avoidance behaviors, as well as modifying the stuttering behavior. Fluency shaping therapy focuses on establishing and generalizing stutter-free speech. Although fluency shaping clinicians do not directly attempt to modify the fears and attitudes of the person who stutters, we suspect that their programs often accomplish this.

These approaches appear to use quite different procedures to develop and maintain fluency. In spite of this, we feel that the post treatment speech of successful clients of these two therapies is often similar. Stuttering modification clinicians tend to use a less structured approach to therapy and to consider as more valid global descriptions of the client's stuttering problem. Fluency shaping clinicians prefer the structure of programmed therapy and tend to collect more objective and reliable data. See Table I on the following page for an overview of the similarities and differences of these two approaches.

TABLE I

Similarities and Differences of Stuttering Modification and Fluency Shaping Therapies

Stuttering Modification Therapy.	Fluency Shaping Therapy.
A. Therapy Goals	**A. Therapy Goals**
1. Considerable attention given to reduction of speech fears and avoidance behaviors.	1. Little attention given to reduction of speech fears and avoidance behaviors.
2. Development of spontaneous fluency, controlled fluency, or acceptable stuttering. Client taught to be more fluent by various techniques to modify his stuttering.	2. Development of spontaneous or controlled fluency. Client taught stutter-free speech in clinical and outside situations.
3. Maintenance of fluency by maintaining reduction of fears and avoidance behaviors. Use of various techniques to modify stuttering.	3. Maintenance of fluency by modifying the manner of speaking, and if necessary, the reinstatement of fluency by recycling through original program. Management of contingencies for stuttering and fluency.
4. Some, but not enough, attention given to general communication skills.	4. Some, but not enough, attention given to general communication skills.
B. Clinical Procedures	**B. Clinical Procedures**
1. Structure is characterized by a teaching/counseling interaction.	1. Structure is characterized by conditioning and programming principles.
2. Data collection in terms of global impression of client's stuttering problem.	2. Data collection in terms of objective data regarding client's speech.

Pros and Cons of Each Approach

The pros and cons of each approach will be considered with regard to the person who stutters, to the clinician, and to the college or university training program. These considerations are important because they can and do affect daily decisions of stutterers and their clinicians. The advantages and disadvantages to the client of each approach will be discussed first.

Stuttering modification therapy is more attractive to some people who stutter because it does not require the stutterer to speak in an abnormal pattern during part of his therapy. On the other hand, some fluency shaping therapy programs do require the person who stutters to use slow prolonged speech for part of their therapy program; and some clients find this manner of speaking rather unpleasant, even though treatment steps ensure that speech naturalness is eventually regained. Thus, stuttering modification therapy would be preferred for this reason by some stutterers.

Stuttering modification therapy, however, does have a real disadvantage on another level. In most stuttering modification therapy the stutterer needs to confront his speech fears. He needs to perform fear-producing tasks. He needs to eliminate his avoidance behaviors and get his stuttering out in the open. Some stutterers find this extremely unpleasant and resist therapy at this point. This resistance can be overcome with the help of an unusually supportive clinician. Unfortunately, however, this skill comes only with considerable experience.

In fluency shaping therapy, however, clients usually are not required to confront their fears as directly as they are in stuttering modification therapy. This is because of its highly structured nature and its gradual sequencing of speech tasks. In these programs, the person who stutters usually confronts his fear in small doses. Thus, many stutterers prefer a fluency shaping therapy approach to confronting fears rather than the stuttering modification approach.

Both approaches also have some pros and cons for the clinician. Stuttering modification therapy tends to be less structured and more spontaneous than fluency shaping therapy. Because of this, the clinician may find it more enjoyable.

Fluency shaping therapy, because of its highly structured nature, can be boring at times. The data collection often used in fluency shaping programs can also be time consuming and laborious. The less structured nature of stuttering modification therapy, however, can be a disadvantage to the clinician, especially the beginning clinician. It involves difficult clinical decisions. Procedures are not laid out in as organized a fashion.

Fluency shaping therapy, on the other hand, because of its highly structured nature requires less insight and less clinical sensitivity. Specific procedures are prescribed as to what to do and when to do it. Also, especially with commercially available programs, there is less planning time needed by the clinician. These two approaches also differ on one other dimension that is of importance to the clinician.

As noted earlier, stuttering modification therapy traditionally has not emphasized the collection of data relative to the stutterer's progress. This may be because the measurement of attitudes and the assessment of the quality of changes in stuttering are difficult. Fluency shaping, however, has placed a great deal of emphasis upon the collection of data. With today's emphasis upon evidence-based practice accountability and treatment outcome assessment, data keeping has become more and more important for the clinician who must write an Individual Education Program (IEP) for each child.

Finally, these therapy approaches have different implications for college and university training programs. It is more difficult to train a student thoroughly in the stuttering modification approach. The student needs to be trained to respond differentially to many more individual differences in their clients. They must learn to provide emotional support at appropriate times.

Although training students in the fluency shaping approach is not without problems, the skills to be taught are more clearly defined and less ambiguous. Table II, on the following page, summarizes the pros and cons of these two approaches to the client, the clinician, and the training program.

TABLE II

Pros and Cons of Stuttering Modification and Fluency Shaping Therapies with regard to: A) Client, B) Clinician, and C) Training Program

Stuttering Modification Therapy.		Fluency Shaping Therapy.	
A. Client		**A. Client**	
PRO	CON	PRO	CON
1. Does not require speaking in abnormal pattern.	1. Needs to confront and perform fear producing tasks.	1. Less need to confront and perform fear producing tasks.	1. May require speaking in abnormal pattern for a period of time.
B. Clinician		**B. Clinician**	
PRO	CON	PRO	CON
1. Therapy tends to be more spontaneous and enjoyable.	1. Therapy is nonstructured, more difficult decisions need to be made.	1. More structured programs available. Thus, less planning needed.	1. Therapy can be boring.
	2. Less data kept for measuring progress for IEP, etc.	2. More data kept for measuring progress for IEP, etc.	2. More charting of data needed.
C. Training Program		**C. Training Program**	
PRO	CON	PRO	CON
	1. More difficult to teach to clinicians.	1. Easier to teach to clinicians.	
		2. There are fewer individual differences, clearer defined decisions based on observed behavior.	

preliminary comments on diagnostic and treatment procedures

Until now, we've been talking in general terms about the goals and procedures of stuttering modification and fluency shaping approaches to therapy with stutterers. In the next three sections of this book, we intend to give many specific suggestions for the diagnosis and treatment of cases. These suggestions, then, will be a guide for the clinician in deciding when and how to use fluency shaping or stuttering modification approaches with stutterers. We will also give suggestions for combining parts of the two approaches.

In the discussion that follows, we have chosen to divide the material by age groups of the clients. Thus, we will be talking about diagnostic and treatment approaches for three age levels: the high school and adult stutterer, the elementary school child who stutters, and the preschool child who stutters. Material pertinent to junior high school children who stutter will be discussed in both the high school/adult section and the elementary school section. Due to the child's maturity and/or stuttering problem, some junior high children would benefit most from treatment procedures described for the high school and adult stutterer. Others would benefit more from procedures described for elementary school children who stutter.

We have chosen to discuss these groups from the oldest to the youngest because we believe that at the high school and adult level the stuttering modification and fluency shaping approaches are the most dissimilar. By beginning at this level, we are able to present more clearly the differences between the two approaches. As we move toward the younger age levels, however, the differences between the two approaches become less pronounced and their similarities become greater.

Even though we discuss stuttering modification therapy and fluency shaping therapy separately, in practice, both of us are advocates of a combined approach.

As we have noted in Chapter I, in some respects the stuttering modification and fluency shaping approaches are similar; both approaches use some similar techniques to develop and maintain fluency. We also feel that each approach has some strengths the other approach does not have.

For example, we believe that the emphasis that stuttering modification approach puts on reduction of fears and avoidances is very important. We attempt to incorporate this into our combined programs. We feel that the stress that fluency shaping approach gives to programming and the collection of data is important. We also like to incorporate these procedures into our combined programs.

Many of the treatment techniques described in this book— both fluency shaping and stuttering modification—are illustrated in the Stuttering Foundation DVD: Basic Clinical Skills.

Chapter 3

the high school
and adult stutterer

This chapter deals primarily with the high school and adult stutterer. More mature or more severe junior high stutterers, however, may benefit from diagnostic and treatment procedures described below. The clinician will need to use her knowledge of the individual child and his problem to decide whether to apply these procedures or those in the chapter on the elementary school child.

Diagnostic Procedures

Feelings and Attitudes

The evaluation of a teen-age or an adult stutterer is primarily an interview accompanied by an exploration and assessment of speech behaviors. From the interview comes, among other things, some idea of the client's feelings and attitudes toward his stuttering. As the stutterer talks, the clinician listens to what the client says as well as how he says it.

We usually begin by asking the stutterer to describe the first memories he has of his stuttering, the changes that took place in his stuttering, and his feelings about it right up to the present. As the client describes the onset and development of his stuttering, we try to understand what he is doing during his moments of stuttering. We also try to assess how he feels about himself by observing body posture, eye contact, facial expressions and other nonverbal cues.

When he has come to a halt in his monologue, we ask questions to fill in any gaps he may have left, such as past treatment or the reactions of parents and friends to his stuttering. In addition, we are interested in the extent to which stuttering interferes with his social, academic and/or vocational adjustment. In this regard, the clinician might want to ask the question, "How would your life change if you became fluent?" The answer may suggest how stuttering may be affecting his life. The clinician may also find out if he expects more from treatment than it can provide.

The high school or adult stutterer also completes the Stutterer's Self Ratings of Reactions to Speech Situations (Darley and Spriestersbach, 1978) and the modified Erickson Scale of Communication Attitudes (Andrews and Cutler, 1974 and Erickson, 1969). If the teen-age stutterer is too young for these questionnaires, we administer the A-19 Scale or the Communication Attitude Test–Revised (Brutten, 1985). The A-19 Scale is reprinted here. Both scales are reprinted in Guitar (2006).

A-19 Scale

Name _____ Date _____

1. Is it best to keep your mouth shut when you are in trouble?   Yes   No

2. When the teacher calls on you, do you get nervous?   Yes   No

3. Do you ask a lot of questions in class?   Yes   No

4. Do you like to talk on the phone?   Yes   No

5. If you did not know a person, would you tell your name?   Yes   No

6. Is it hard to talk to your teacher?   Yes   No

7. Would you go up to a new boy or girl in your class?   Yes   No

8. Is it hard to keep control of your voice when talking?   Yes   No

9. Even when you know the right answer, are you afraid to say it?   Yes   No

10. Do you like to tell other children what to do?   Yes   No

11. Is it fun to talk to your dad?   Yes   No

12. Do you like to tell stories to your classmates?   Yes   No

13. Do you wish you could say things as clearly as the other kids do?   Yes   No

14. Would you rather look at a comic book than talk to a friend?   Yes   No

15. Are you upset when someone interrupts you?   Yes   No

16. When you want to say something, do you just say it?   Yes   No

17. Is talking to your friends more fun than playing by yourself?   Yes   No

18. Are you sometimes unhappy?   Yes   No

19. Are you a little afraid to talk on the phone?   Yes   No

A-19 Scale for Children Who Stutter

Susan Andre and Barry Guitar
University of Vermont

Establish rapport with the child, and make sure that he or she is physically comfortable before beginning administration. Explain the task to the child and make sure he or she understands what is required. Some simple directions might be used:

"I am going to ask you some questions. Listen carefully and then tell me what you think:

Yes or No. There is no right or wrong answer. I just want to know what you think.

To begin the scale, ask the questions in a natural manner. Do not urge the child to respond before he or she is ready, and repeat the question if the child did not hear it or you feel that he or she did not understand it. Do not re-word the question unless you feel it is absolutely necessary, and then write the question you asked under that item.

Circle the answer that corresponds to the child's response. Be accepting of the child's response because there is no right or wrong answer. If all the child will say is "I don't know" even after prompting, record that response next to the question.

For the younger children (kindergarten and first grade), it might be necessary to give a few simple examples to ensure comprehension of the required task:

    a. Are you a boy?   Yes   No

    b. Do you have black hair?   Yes   No

Similar, obvious questions may be inserted, if necessary, to reassure the examiner that the child is actively cooperating at all times. Adequately praise the child for listening and assure him or her that a good job is being done.

It is important to be familiar with the questions so that they can be read in a natural manner.

The child is given 1 point for each answer that matches those given below. The higher a child's score, the more probable it is that he or she has developed negative attitudes toward communication. In our study, the mean score of the K through 4th grade stutterers (N = 28) was 9.07 (S.D. = 2.44), and for the 28 matched controls, it was 8.17 (S.D. = 1.80).

Score 1 point for each answer that matches these:

1. Yes	6. Yes	11. No	16. No
2. Yes	7. No	12. No	17. No
3. No	8. Yes	13. Yes	18. Yes
4. No	9. Yes	14. Yes	19. Yes
5. No	10. No	15. Yes	

A-19 Scale

Name _____ Date _____

1. Is it best to keep your mouth shut when you are in trouble?   Yes

No

2. When the teacher calls on you, do you get nervous?   Yes

No

3. Do you ask a lot of questions in class?   Yes

No

4. Do you like to talk on the phone?   Yes

No

5. If you did not know a person, would you tell your name?   Yes

No

6. Is it hard to talk to your teacher?   Yes

No

7. Would you go up to a new boy or girl in your class?   Yes

No

8. Is it hard to keep control of your voice when talking?   Yes

No

9. Even when you know the right answer, are you afraid to say it?   Yes

No

10. Do you like to tell other children what to do?   Yes

No

11. Is it fun to talk to your dad?   Yes

A-19 Scale for Children Who Stutter

Susan Andre and Barry Guitar
University of Vermont

Establish rapport with the child, and make sure that he or she is physically comfortable before beginning administration. Explain the task to the child and make sure he or she understands what is required. Some simple directions might be used:

"I am going to ask you some questions. Listen carefully and then tell me what you think:

Yes or No. There is no right or wrong answer. I just want to know what you think.

To begin the scale, ask the questions in a natural manner. Do not urge the child to respond before he or she is ready, and repeat the question if the child did not hear it or you feel that he or she did not understand it. Do not re-word the question unless you feel it is absolutely necessary, and then write the question you asked under that item.

Circle the answer that corresponds to the child's response. Be accepting of the child's response because there is no right or wrong answer. If all the child will say is "I don't know" even after prompting, record that response next to the question.

For the younger children (kindergarten and first grade), it might be necessary to give a few simple examples to ensure comprehension of the required task:

a. Are you a boy?	Yes	No
b. Do you have black hair?	Yes	No

Similar, obvious questions may be inserted, if necessary, to reassure the examiner that the child is actively cooperating at all times. Adequately praise the child for listening and assure him or her that a good job is being done.

It is important to be familiar with the questions so that they can be read in a natural manner.

The child is given 1 point for each answer that matches those given below. The higher a child's score, the more probable it is that he or she has developed negative attitudes toward communication. In our study, the mean score of the K through 4th grade stutterers (N = 28) was 9.07 (S.D. = 2.44), and for the 28 matched controls, it was 8.17 (S.D. = 1.80).

Score 1 point for each answer that matches these:

1. Yes	6. Yes	11. No	16. No
2. Yes	7. No	12. No	17. No
3. No	8. Yes	13. Yes	18. Yes
4. No	9. Yes	14. Yes	19. Yes
5. No	10. No	15. Yes	

Speech Behaviors

Next, we talk to the stutterer about some relatively neutral topic, such as his job or school. We tape record this, getting at least five minutes of his conversational speech. We recommend videotaping speech samples to permit more valid assessment of the client's changes in his stuttering. If video is unavailable, audiotape can be used. We also tape five minutes of his oral reading.

Later, using the tape recording, we count stuttering behaviors and measure speech rate. We strongly urge the clinician to measure the stuttering frequency and speech rate during the diagnostic evaluation. This will give a baseline of behavior to compare with the progress demonstrated by the client at the termination of therapy.

These behavioral measures do not capture all the important aspects of the stuttering, but they are valuable in preparing progress reports and in helping assess the effectiveness of therapy. They are also helpful in preparing Individual Education Programs (IEPs). Stuttering frequency can be measured as either the number of stuttered words per minute (SW/M) or percent stuttered syllables (% SS). If the clinician is measuring only stuttering frequency, it may be easier to count stuttered words per minute. If she is also measuring speech rate as well as stuttering frequency, percent syllables stuttered and syllables per minute is easier.[1]

Although measuring stuttering frequency and speech rate is easily done from a tape recording, these measures do not adequately assess the stuttering of those who stutter less frequently but with severe blocks. A more complete assessment of all stutterers requires some measure of severity. The Scale for Rating Severity of Stuttering (Darley and Spriestersbach, 1978)

---

[1]The clinician can count stuttered words or syllables easily using a mini-calculator. Most mini-calculators that cost under ten dollars allow you to count cumulatively by pressing "1," then pressing the "+," after which the "=" is pressed repeatedly, once for each behavior to be counted. A cumulative total will appear on the readout. Frequency of stuttering is usually assessed by percentage of syllables stuttered. This percentage can be obtained by dividing the total number of stutters by total number of syllables spoken. Speech rate can be assessed by measuring the stutterer's speaking time with a stopwatch and counting the number of syllables spoken during this period of time. Speaking time is simply the time the speaker is actually talking, so pauses greater than two seconds are excluded. Speech rate is obtained by dividing total syllables by speaking time.

and the Stuttering Severity Instrument (Riley,1994) are useful for this purpose. In order to measure severity it is necessary to make the assessments while the stutterer is talking and reading or from a videotape.

There are other aspects of the stutterer's speech behaviors that give important diagnostic clues. If reading produces more stuttering than conversation, we suspect that in conversing the client is substituting easier words for those likely to be stuttered. We also scrutinize the client's speech in conversation to see if he uses fillers, postponements, starters or other tricks to appear normally fluent. In general we try to assess the extent to which the stutterer is avoiding stuttering. This helps us to decide the course of treatment.

Trial Therapy

When the clinician has completed her assessment of the client's attitudes about his stuttering and the frequency and severity of it, she should introduce some trial therapy procedures. We want to get an idea how the stutterer would respond to some stuttering modification procedures. He is asked to read a passage and instructed to stutter as openly as possible. His ability to stutter openly is rewarded with approval. Next, we instruct him to continue to stutter openly but to stutter more easily and with less tension and struggle. We determine if his stuttering becomes milder as he reads and follows these modification procedures. These results give us insight into how he will respond to stuttering modification therapy.

We are also interested in the client's response to fluency shaping. We have found slow prolonged speech among the easiest of the fluency shaping approaches to administer for trial therapy. Basically, this is the program described by Perkins (1973); a more recent version of this approach can be found in O'Brian, S., Onslow, M., Cream, A. & Packman, A. (2003). Camperdown Program: Outcomes of a new prolonged-speech treatment model.

---

[1] Since a DAF machine will cost several hundred dollars, it may be prohibitive from a budgetary point of view for one clinician. However, where a number of clinicians are employed by the same agency or school district, it is easy to share the use of one DAF machine. The authors have seen this work effectively in a number of situations. For more information, visit www.stutteringhelp.org.

Journal of Speech, Language, and Hearing Research, 46, 933-946. This can be done with or without Delayed Auditory Feedback (DAF).[1] When DAF is used, the machine is set at 250 millisecond delay and the clinician models prolonged speech in which words are uttered in very slow motion.

With the aid of DAF the client imitates the clinician. The initial sounds of the words must be said extremely slowly. If the rate of utterance is slow enough, no stuttering will occur. In trial therapy, the stutterer goes through the alphabet, saying a single word beginning with each letter. If stuttering occurs, he is re-instructed to utter the word more slowly, particularly the first sounds of the word. Once all twenty-six words are said fluently, the stutterer is asked to read a paragraph using slow prolonged speech. The client then answers simple questions with complete sentences using slow prolonged speech. The clinician will want to note how fluent he is as well as how he reacts to using slow speech.

These same procedures can be used without a DAF machine by the clinician modeling the slow prolonged pattern. Everything else would be similar to the procedures described above with the DAF machine.[1] At this point the interview is complete. The following sections tell how to use this information to prescribe treatment.

Indications for Stuttering Modification Therapy

Feelings and Attitudes

Stuttering modification therapy would be appropriate for a stutterer who fits the following description. His pattern of development of stuttering would suggest that he suffers a fair amount of penalty for stuttering. He would indicate that life is pretty miserable when he stutters. More than likely, parents, friends, teachers and others are not overly accepting of his stuttering. In addition, the clinician's impression of his present situation would be that he is very uncomfortable with his stuttering; and he feels it is holding him back from things he would like to do.

---

[1]Slow prolonged speech without the DAF machine is described more fully in this chapter when we discuss therapy procedures for the combined approach.

Further indications for the stuttering modification approach include high scores on the modified Erickson Scale of Communication Attitudes (for example, 19/24 or higher); and on the Avoidance section of the Stutterers Self Ratings of Reactions to Speech Situations (for example, a mean of 2.50 or above). These cut-off scores are based on a study (Guitar, 1976) of pre-treatment measures of stutterers' attitudes and post-treatment measures of stutterers' speech behaviors. Because these scores are based on a small sample treated by a single approach (fluency shaping) they should be regarded as preliminary estimates. We encourage others to gather and share with us such data on other stutterers.

Speech Behaviors

The stuttering modification approach is neither indicated nor contraindicated by the severity of the stuttering. This approach works as well with mild as with severe stutterers. The important thing to consider is how much the stutterer avoids or hides his stuttering. If he spends considerable energy disguising his stuttering, he is more likely to profit from stuttering modification therapy.

Trial Therapy

Stuttering modification therapy may be indicated if the stutterer's severity or struggle behaviors become milder during stuttering modification trial therapy procedures. We suspect that if this happens it is because the stutterer is attempting to avoid stuttering less or is able to confront his fear of stuttering. Both of these are aspects of stuttering modification therapy.

Stuttering modification therapy would be even more strongly indicated if, in addition to showing the improvement described above, the stutterer has difficulty producing fluent speech in the fluency shaping trial therapy. If, however, fluency is produced, but the stutterer finds slow prolonged speech uncomfortable, stuttering modification therapy may also be indicated.

In summary, the factors that would suggest a stuttering modification approach would be relatively strong negative feelings and attitudes toward stuttering and positive change during stuttering modification trial therapy. Moreover, stuttering modification therapy would be indicated if the stutterer does not respond well to fluency shaping trial therapy. The severity of the stuttering would not be significant, but the extent of avoidance behavior, however measured, would be important for deciding to use stuttering modification therapy.

Indications for Fluency Shaping Therapy

Feelings and Attitudes

The fluency shaping approach would be effective with those whose stuttering is not maintained by strong negative emotions. This stutterer is likely to be talkative during the interview, will describe his stuttering as having begun with easy repetitions. In time, his stuttering may have grown more severe, but never so severe that it kept him from talking. His parents and friends have accepted him. His stuttering annoys him and may interfere a little with his life but is not a great handicap to him. The Erickson Scale score will likely be low, for example, 13/24 or less, and the mean Avoidance score will probably be below 2.50.

Speech Behaviors

The severity and frequency of the client's stuttering may vary. A good candidate for fluency shaping, however, will not go to great lengths to disguise his stuttering. His stuttering will be easily observable when he has it.

Trial Therapy

This stutterer will be comfortable with prolonged speech during fluency shaping trial therapy; and by using it, he will find that even conversational fluency comes easily.

In summary, we feel that fluency shaping procedures would be very effective when the client has relatively low communication attitude and avoidance scores and responds well to slow prolonged speech during trial fluency shaping therapy. This would be true regardless of the severity of the stuttering, and especially true when there is minimal avoidance behavior.

Indications for Combined Therapy

In our experience most clients will benefit from a combination of stuttering modification and fluency shaping approaches at some stage of their treatment. We believe this for the following reasons. We think that fluency shaping therapy is more efficient than stuttering modification therapy for changing speech patterns. We also think, however, that stuttering modification therapy is more effective in reducing speech fears and improving speech attitudes for those clients who need it.

The combined approaches we describe here are not necessarily the only ways these two approaches can be combined. There are an infinite variety of ways to combine them. We present only the ways we have combined stuttering modification and fluency shaping therapies with the same client. We suspect other clinicians have combined these approaches in other ways.

Feelings and Attitudes

Many times we encounter high school or adult stutterers who have characteristics that point toward both the stuttering modification and fluency shaping approaches. In general, stutterers who are good candidates for a combined approach will be those who have some fear of stuttering but not the morbidity of some severe stutterers who have taken their rejections and penalties deeply to heart. Their Erickson Scale and Avoidance scores will usually be in the moderate range.

Speech Behaviors

The severity and frequency of stuttering may vary considerably in the candidate for the combined approach, but this client's speech is likely to contain evidence of avoidance (e.g., circumlocutions, postponements and starters). As we mentioned in the description of our diagnostic procedures, we compare reading and talking and we scan the stutterer's speech for evidence of attempts to hide stuttering.

Trial Therapy

A combined approach may be indicated when the stutterer responds somewhat favorably to both stuttering modification or fluency shaping trial therapies. That approach, which results in the most positive response, may be the best starting place in the treatment program. This would increase the probability of initial success. As the need to work on the other aspect of the problem becomes apparent, this need would be met later in the program by implementation of the other approach.

In summary, a stutterer may be a good candidate for a combined approach when he exhibits needs that can most effectively be met by both approaches. This client may have negative emotions about stuttering and avoid words and situations, but these components of his problem are not overwhelming. This stutterer exhibits a generally positive response to both trial therapies. Our experience suggests that most clients fit this description and most would be suited for a combined approach.

Treatment Procedures

Stuttering Modification Therapy

Perhaps more has been written about stuttering modification treatment with adult stutterers than about all other treatments. We won't try to cover the ground that has been covered so well by others. We recommend the book *Therapy for Stutterers* (1974). In addition, the videotape series by Van Riper (1974)[1] will give you models to follow. It is our experience that most effective stuttering modification therapy is done by clinicians who experiment with variations of the approach, inventing their own activities, taking some ideas from one author, some from another, and finally coming up with a blend that suits their own personality.

---

[1]This videotape series with a 20-year followup now is available in DVD format (2007) from the Stuttering Foundation of America, 1-800-992-9392, www.stutteringhelp.org.

The two critical elements in stuttering modification therapy for adults are: 1) decreasing the stutterer's speech fears and avoidance behaviors, and 2) teaching the person who stutters that by reducing the physical tension when attempting a feared word or sound he can stutter more easily and speak with less abnormality. These two elements interact. If the clinician is able to provide activities and an environment in which the stutterer can experiment with a fearless attitude toward stuttering, his stuttering will become milder. In addition, if she can demonstrate to the client how to stutter in ways that do not recoil from the moment of helplessness and he can emulate her model, he will feel his blocks release a little sooner and his feeling of helplessness will decrease.

Knowing how and when to guide the stutterer into attitude change or behavior change takes some talent. Reading and re-reading descriptions of stuttering modification therapy and watching videotapes (for example, "If You Stutter: Advice for Adults," Guitar & Guitar, 1998) will help the clinician develop this talent. Then she must work with as many stutterers as she can. Experience and interest are the best teachers.

Case History

Patricia is an attractive young lady of 24. Her husband convinced her to seek treatment for her stuttering since it was interfering with both her job as a secretary and her social life. She stuttered with a great deal of facial contortions and would even protrude her tongue on long blocks. Although there were situations where she could talk easily, her stuttering was severe when she talked with her boss or anyone else whom she perceived as an authority figure. She felt totally helpless during moments of stuttering and deeply ashamed afterwards. Patricia's score on the Erickson Scale was 18/24 and her mean score on the Avoidance section of the Stutterer's Self Ratings of Reactions to Speech Situations was 3.00.

In trial therapy, when Patricia spoke on the DAF machine, she could be fluent at the slowest rate, but she said she was bothered by the droning sound of her voice and by the headphones. When we modeled a less monotonous style of prolonged speech and asked her to try this without the DAF machine, she quickly found herself in her old trigger postures at the beginnings of some words.

While it might have been possible to develop fluency through the use of the DAF machine, Patricia's avoidance behaviors and attitudes, with her sensitivity to penalty, suggested a stuttering modification approach would be more effective in the long run.

Patricia's treatment followed the pattern of adult stuttering modification therapy described by Van Riper (1973, 1974), Manning (2001), Shapiro (1999), and Conture (2001). We began by helping her understand that she had the responsibility for managing her stuttering, possibly a life-long task. With her help we developed assignments for her to talk to people at work about her stuttering. At the time she was doing this, we helped her to explore her own stuttering in the safety of the treatment room. We tried to help her learn, at an emotional level, that when she looked at stuttering as if she were examining a spider, piece by piece, it became much less of a fearsome thing.

We took her out into a variety of public situations and demonstrated that we could fake stuttering without becoming upset. Gradually, she was able to do this herself, first with us along, and then alone. When she had been successful with fake stuttering, we guided her through experiences in calmly analyzing what she was doing in moments of stuttering she had while at work. She learned to stay in the moment of stuttering and reduce the physical tension she had been using to try to force her way out of the block. In this part of the treatment we saw significant changes in Patricia's attitudes. She seemed to be seeking out stuttering instead of avoiding it.

In this section of therapy, we also included plenty of reinforcement for easier stuttering in Patricia's speech. Unlike many stutterers, Patricia did not find her stuttering getting worse as she analyzed it and stuttered more openly. Nevertheless, we warned her that this might happen and that such an occurrence, while unpleasant, would be entirely natural. Perhaps our warning forestalled this.

Once Patricia's attitude was clearly one of interest and approach toward stuttering, we took her through the three steps of cancellations, pull-outs and preparatory sets. For Patricia, her own real curiosity about her stuttering behavior seemed to carry her rapidly through these steps. After eleven treatment sessions,

Patricia was stuttering markedly less in all situations and enjoyed working through her blocks when they occurred. After a semester's treatment, Patricia discontinued therapy saying she was ready to work by herself.

Several months after she stopped treatment, Patricia called us and requested some temporary help. She was beginning to slip back a bit into hard blocks. We repeated some of our earlier desensitization procedures, based on our analysis of the difficulty she was having. As she worked on faking stuttering while remaining calm and on analyzing her blocks, she recognized her need for continued fear reduction. She regained the fluency she had after her initial treatment and continues to do well today.

Fluency Shaping Therapy

In recent years a number of speech-language pathologists have been writing about fluency shaping programs. To give the reader a feeling for this approach, we will present a typical fluency shaping program and discuss its application with one of our clients. In designing this program we were particularly influenced by the writings of Ryan (2001). The reader may also wish to consult Curlee & Siegel (1996) and Curlee (1999) for other descriptions of fluency shaping programs.

Ryan (2001) divides therapy into three stages: establishment, transfer, and maintenance. The goal of the establishment stage is to establish fluency in the stutterer's speech in the clinical setting. Several different procedures or programs are used to accomplish this. We will describe a delayed auditory feedback (DAF) program for establishing fluency. The goal of the transfer stage of the program is to transfer or generalize the client's fluency to everyday speaking situations. The maintenance phase of the program is concerned with retaining the fluency over time.

In the establishment and transfer stages, tasks are sequenced from easy to hard. The client is socially reinforced for fluency all along the way. To progress from one step to the next the client must meet certain criteria in terms of number of stuttered words per unit of time. To give the reader a better appreciation of this approach we will describe our therapy approach with Jim, one of our clients.

Case History

Jim was a university student with severe overt stuttering. He had few word or situation avoidances. His attitude toward stuttering was rather accepting. He was frustrated by his stuttering, but he did not allow it to keep him from leading a very active social life. His score on the Erickson Scale was 12, which is low for adult stutterers. He responded very well to trial therapy on the DAF machine.

We began therapy with Jim reading in a slow, prolonged fluent pattern on the DAF machine. The machine was set at 250 millisecond (ms.) delay. At this setting the stutterer speaks only 30-40 words per minute. After Jim had read fluently for half an hour at this 250 ms. rate, the DAF machine was set at 200 ms. delay. Now Jim could read a little faster, and another half hour of fluency was obtained. The DAF machine was again changed; this time to 150 ms. delay, and Jim read for another half hour without stuttering. This pattern was followed through delays of 100, 50 and 0 ms. In this way Jim's fluent reading was gradually increased from a slow prolonged pattern into a pattern that sounded normal and was within normal rates. This was accomplished over several therapy sessions.

This same sequence was then repeated but with Jim speaking in monologue rather than reading. Then it was done a third time with Jim and the clinician engaged in conversation. Thus, by going through various speaking rates (delay times on the DAF) and three different speaking modes (reading, monologue and conversation), we arrived at a point where Jim was speaking fluently with the clinician in the therapy room. This ended the establishment stage of the program. Next came transfer.

In the transfer phase we set up three hierarchies for Jim. The first was a site hierarchy. Jim and the clinician went into seven or eight different physical settings (arranged from easy to hard by Jim) and conversed for a half hour. Jim's goal again was to maintain his fluency talking to the clinician. If he stuttered more than criterion levels allowed, we went back to the previous step and repeated it.

Next we set up a social hierarchy. In this hierarchy Jim and the clinician met with more and more people, and Jim's task was to maintain his fluency in each of these situations. First, we brought in one more person, then two people, and finally we built up to an audience of a dozen.

The last hierarchy involved outside speaking situations that Jim had to complete on his own. This hierarchy consisted of 45 speaking situations, ranked from easy to hard that Jim entered on his own. He had to successfully maintain his fluency in each situation before he progressed to the next one. Jim completed all 45 situations. We had now completed the transfer program. By this time Jim was speaking fluently in all one-to-one situations and speaking with only minimal stuttering in group situations. Approximately three months had elapsed since Jim's program began.

He was now put on a maintenance program. Our contacts with Jim became systematically further and further apart. Jim continued doing a lot of talking, especially in difficult situations, and reported only a little stuttering. He reported being fluent in his easy situations. When the time came for Jim to graduate from the university, we gave him a supply of postcards and asked him to write to us every few months. He did this for several years, and his fluency was maintained at the same level. Then we lost contact with Jim.

Combined Therapy

High school and adult stutterers who are best suited for a combined approach will benefit from both stuttering modification and fluency shaping therapies. We are still experimenting with ways to sequence these approaches when they are combined. In this section, we present a sequence in which fluency shaping treatment is followed by stuttering modification treatment. Another way of sequencing them may be just as good, as the combined therapy section on the elementary school stutterer suggests.

The fluency shaping procedures described in Curlee & Siegel (1996) and Conture & Curlee (2007) work well in the combined approach. In the following paragraphs we describe a modification of these procedures which can be used for fluency shaping without a DAF machine.

The establishment of normal-sounding fluent speech in the treatment room is the first goal of this combined approach. In achieving this goal, the clinician will need to begin by having the stutterer speak entirely fluently, albeit slowly, for five minutes. To guarantee fluency, have the stutterer use the same slow prolonged speech used in the first step of the DAF fluency shaping program discussed earlier. Teach him the proper quality of prolonged speech by selecting a passage 40 syllables in length and reading it aloud so slowly that it takes a full minute to finish it.

First, model the speech for him and then ask him to read the passage. Achieve the proper slow rate not by pausing between words, but by stretching each vowel and each consonant. Vowels are easy to stretch. Consonants are harder. Stretching will distort stops and affricates, but don't worry. This distortion will keep voice and airflow coming, making it difficult to stutter.

In addition to being slow, the speech at the beginning of the program should be relaxed; moreover, voice and/or air should flow out smoothly, without interruption, for each short phrase that can be said on one breath. Work on this quality and rate of speech with the stutterer until satisfied that it is smooth, relaxed and very fluent.

If it is properly produced, anything the stutterer says with this sort of speech will be absolutely fluent. If we seem to be belaboring the point, it is only because the quality of fluency at the beginning influences whether or not the client will maintain fluency in the long term.

The first goal in this combined program is for the client to speak in conversational speech to the clinician, for five minutes, using slow prolonged speech. This must be entirely fluent. If he stutters, re-instruct him and model for him the proper type of speech and reset the stopwatch to zero. Once he has been clocked for five full minutes of fluent conversational speech at this rate he is ready to move up the establishment hierarchy.

We might add here that in order to monitor rate the clinician may want to use a mini-calculator to count syllables in the manner described in the diagnostic section of this chapter. If she prefers to quantify speech rate by words rather than syllables, she can multiply the syllables per minute rates by 0.7 to get a rough estimate of the word per minute rate.

Using the prolonged speech approach, the subsequent goals for the establishment phase are in terms of the rate of speech. After the stutterer has succeeded in reaching the 40 syllables per minute goal, the next goal is set at 45 syllables a minute. Again, the clinician may wish to develop a model of this rate by finding a 45-syllable passage to read in exactly one minute. When she has the proper rate for this passage, she should record it and save it as a model for the 45 syllables per minute rate. She should do this with passages she reads at each five syllable per minute increment until she has reached 180 syllables per minute. In other words, she will have 29 one-minute recordings: one at 40 syllables per minute, one at 45, one at 50, etc., up to 180 syllables per minute.

Use the recordings mentioned above to set the pace for each five minute trial with the client. Be sure the beginning sound in each phrase is extremely slow and that each consonant is as extended as each vowel, even though this will result in some distortion of consonants. If the clinician is using the proper kind of prolonged speech, the stutterer should have almost no trouble retaining fluency until he has reached about 120 syllables per minute. When he reaches this rate, proceed carefully, re-doing trials when stutters occur.

As long as relatively few problems occur, continue progressing up the prolonged speech hierarchy until the client reaches 180 syllables per minute, or until the client's rate sounds normal. Study the article by Perkins (1973) and the chapter by Neilson (1999) to learn the finer points of shaping prolonged speech.

When normal-sounding prolonged speech is achieved, use the generalization procedures described in the section on fluency shaping treatment in this chapter or refer to the excellent generalization procedures in Ryan's book (2001) or the article by Neilson (1999). The strategy used in all generalization is to have the client use the new behavior in situations that are more and more like his everyday life. Start with easier situations and gradually move to situations that are more like the client's difficult life situations. The progression should be done as briskly and as diligently as possible.

Confidence in one situation will carry over in approaching the next if minimal time is lost between attempts. If failure occurs, the clinician must take the client back and repeat the last successful step. This will reinstate mastery of the new behavior and will rebuild confidence before the new step is attempted again.

In a combined approach, the fluency shaping can be done either on an intensive schedule or on a typical two-sessions per week schedule. One of the authors has worked with many clients on an intensive (six to eight hours per day for two days) schedule for fluency shaping. He finds that this option provides great motivation at the outset of therapy because fluency is established so rapidly. The use of intensive scheduling with younger stutterers will be discussed in the next chapter.

Once fluency is established and transferred, the combined approach uses stuttering modification procedures to help the stutterer retain fluency. We use the role therapy of Sheehan (1970) for some of the stuttering modification activities. This involves telling friends and colleagues that you are a stutterer working on your speech. This kind of open attitude seems to be considerably easier for a stutterer once he has achieved substantial fluency.

Other stuttering modification activities can be taken from the section entitled "Calming and Toughening the Stutterer" in the book *Therapy for Stutterers* (1974), the book by Manning (2001) and the videotape *If You Stutter: Advice for Adults* (Guitar & Guitar, 1998) and Helliesen, G. (2006). *Speech Therapy for the Severe Older Adolescent and Adult Stutterer: A Program for Change*. Newport News, VA.: Apollo Press. Available from www.apollopress.com

Case History

Judy is a 29-year-old architectural draftswoman who referred herself for treatment of a moderately severe stutter. Prior to coming to us, she had been through brief hypnotherapy by a psychologist who sought to cure her stuttering this way. Under hypnosis Judy had explored the beginnings of her stuttering and a number of traumatic events relating to it.

Although this gave her some insight into the presumed onset of the problem, her speech behavior was unaffected. In the diagnostic interview Judy's stuttering frequency was 11% SS; she had obvious stuttering blocks characterized by considerable struggle and facial contortion. Her Erickson score was 18/24 and her Avoidance score was 3.50.

Judy was first treated with an intensive (two-day) fluency shaping approach. Early in the DAF treatment she told us that the DAF headphones were bothering her and we did the remainder of the treatment without DAF, using control of speech rate, as described above. By the end of the second day, Judy was entirely fluent and had progressed through a transfer hierarchy consisting of many interviews with strangers, phone conversations with friends and with storekeepers, and a speech to an audience of fifteen.

The following day she went back to work and at our urging described her stuttering problem and her recent treatment to friends and colleagues. In addition, Judy enlisted their help in listening for stutters and for rapid speech in her conversations. She also tape recorded many of her conversations and analyzed them with the clinician on subsequent visits.

After four or five weekly sessions following the intensive treatment, Judy dismissed herself from therapy. Phone calls at six and twelve months and two years after treatment indicate Judy is maintaining controlled fluency with an occasional, acceptable mild stutter.

Indications for Change in Approaches

There will be times when a therapy program with a given high school student or adult isn't going well. If the clinician has tried a given approach to the best of her ability for a reasonable period of time, and if the client has not made gains during this period, then it would be reasonable to try another approach.

There may be many reasons for the failure of a given approach with a particular client, most of which the clinician will never be able to determine. Expect to make mistakes, accept them, and be willing to change. It is important, though, that the clinician recognize when her client is no longer making progress and that she shift gears at this time. In the following sections we will discuss some of the more frequent problems we have had and what we have done about them.

Changing From a Stuttering Modification Approach

The most frequent problem we have had with stutterers in stuttering modification therapy programs is their resistance in confronting their speech fears. This is usually manifested by the stutterer either quitting therapy or by only token involvement in the therapy process. At this point we have found it helpful to change to a fluency shaping program or to a combined program.

We explain to the stutterer that this new approach will whittle away at his speech fears in little steps. We indicate that in the long run he will get to the same place, but will take a different route. At this point, we will change to a slow prolonged speech program and work up through a hierarchy. See our earlier discussion of Judy.

Changing From a Fluency Shaping Approach

The most frequent problems we find with fluency shaping programs is that they fail in the later stages of generalization or in the maintenance of fluency. The problems seem to be of two types. The first is that the stutterer still has considerable fear of certain speaking situations, despite the fact that we have approached them through a graded hierarchy of successively more fearful situations. When he approaches these situations his fear becomes too great, and he is unable to maintain his fluency. In these cases we have found it helpful to go to a combined approach. What the stutterer needs for a time now are some desensitization activities from the stuttering modification approach. These could include such activities as talking to people about his stuttering, and perhaps fake stuttering.

The second problem that we have encountered in fluency shaping programs is that the stutterer does not have any coping techniques to deal with anticipated or actual stuttering in everyday speaking situations. He can be either fluent or he will stutter; he has no way to deal with his moments of stuttering. We have found it helpful at these times to go to a combined approach. We must help the stutterer feel that it is acceptable to stutter. We will then teach him some technique, such as pull-out or a preparatory set, to handle the stuttering when it occurs.

Fluency Maintaining Strategies

Once the client has achieved a high level of fluency, termination of therapy should be considered. It should also be considered when the client is happy with his speech and no longer feels the need to continue therapy. Whatever the reasons, all formal therapy programs come to an end, and stutterers have to fly on their own.

Adult stutterers are notorious for relapsing. Most speech-language pathologists have had the opportunity of watching one of their successful clients slip back to the pre-therapy level of disfluency. This is disappointing, both for the clinician and the stutterer—especially for the stutterer. In this section we will discuss what you and the stutterer can do to maintain his new fluency level. We will do this first from the stuttering modification therapy point of view.

Stuttering Modification Therapy

Once again we would refer you to some references we mentioned earlier. We believe that the book *Therapy for Stutterers* (1974) would be helpful to you. We also believe Van Riper's chapter on "Stabilization" in his *The Treatment of Stuttering* (Van Riper, 1973) and the books by Manning (2001) and Shapiro (1999) are an excellent source for ideas on maintaining fluency.

Earlier we defined three levels of fluency: spontaneous fluency, controlled fluency and acceptable stuttering. We believe the fluency maintaining strategies for each of these levels are similar, but some small differences between them make it worthwhile to discuss the strategies for each separately.

To maintain spontaneous fluency it is important that your client keep his speech fears at an extremely low level. He should also have eliminated-and keep eliminated-all avoidance behaviors. That is, he should not avoid any words or situations. What he should do is as much talking as possible. He should seek out situations he fears and keeps entering them until he is no longer afraid. He may continue to do this for years following therapy. The clinician helps him understand that he will need to maintain his reduction of speech fears and avoidance behaviors on his own for many years to come.

Most stutterers, however, will not be spontaneously fluent forever, but will have small temporary relapses and exhibit stuttering from time to time. In this case they will need skills to maintain controlled fluency.

In controlled fluency the person pays attention to his speech to maintain normal sounding fluency. He may monitor his speech rate. He may pay attention to the sound of his speech or to the movements involved in speaking. He may use pull-outs and preparatory sets. Whatever techniques he uses, he will have to be good at them, and this will take time and practice. During therapy, the clinician convinces him of the need for maintaining his speech control skills and maintaining reduced speech fears and avoidances.

Finally, if your client is to maintain acceptable stuttering, rather than spontaneous or controlled fluency, he will need to employ the same strategies as we discussed above. His residual stuttering will remain at a tolerable level only if he continues to accept his stuttering and does not try to avoid it.

Fluency Shaping Therapy

If the fluency shaping program has succeeded, and the client's fluency has generalized to all speaking situations in his life, the goal is to maintain this level of fluency. Spontaneous fluency is maintained by talking as much as possible in these situations and by self-reinforcement. If the client begins to stutter, he uses whatever speech control techniques he learned during his treatment. For example, he might slow his speaking rate for situations in which he anticipates stuttering. He may also repeat some of the same steps he went through in his original program. In this way the client could maintain controlled fluency.

The clinician makes sure that the client understands what program steps to repeat to use controls to maintain fluency. Furthermore, by frequently reassessing his own speech behaviors, the client is motivated to maintain his gains. We recommend the article by Hanna and Owen (1977) and fluency-shaping chapters in Conture & Curlee (2007) for further maintenance strategies.

Combined Approach

For maintaining fluency in a combined approach, we rely on stuttering modification strategies. It is important for the stutterer to keep his speech fears and avoidances at a low level. Even when our clients have developed near-perfect fluency after the fluency shaping component of combined therapy, we have them fake stutter with inner calmness in a variety of speaking situations. It is also important for the stutterer to have some way to handle moments of stuttering when they occur.

Chapter 4

the elementary school child who stutters

The diagnostic and treatment procedures described in this chapter are primarily for the elementary school child. Many junior high school stutterers, however, may benefit more from these procedures than those in the preceding chapter. This is especially true for junior high school children who are less mature or whose stuttering is milder. The decision is one that needs to be made by the clinician.

Diagnostic Procedures

Feelings and Attitudes

Diagnostic procedures vary depending on whether or not the youngster's parents are present at the evaluation and on the severity of the stuttering. Since these children are usually identified in a school setting, we typically see them before we talk to their parents.

The starting point for evaluation is a conversation with the child in the treatment room. We talk about hobbies and summer vacation, as well as likes and dislikes, particularly in school. If the child is stuttering with struggle and tension, we comment about his stuttering in a neutral way and try to elicit some feelings or comments about it from him. We might say, for example, "Some of those words are pretty hard, aren't they?" Our goal is to put him at ease. We want him to feel comfortable with us so that we can begin to develop a working relationship. We also want to get a true picture of his feelings about his stuttering. We explore with him how much his stuttering keeps him from talking when he wants to. We also ask what he thinks his parents think about his stuttering.

If he is talkative, if his body language is relaxed but expressive, if he discusses his stuttering without evident shame or avoidance, if he seems to genuinely feel his stuttering doesn't bother his parents, he probably has few negative feelings about his stuttering. More information on this topic can be gathered by administering the A-19 Scale or Communication Attitude Test–Revised (Brutten, 1985).

The most effective treatment for this age group involves the parents as well as the stutterer. This means you will talk to his parents after you have assessed your young client. In talking with the parents, we try to get a complete description of the development of the child's stuttering, as well as his current behaviors and attitudes.

From talking with the parents, the clinician can get an idea if and how much they penalize the child's stuttering either overtly or covertly. How do they feel about the stuttering? How do they respond to it? Do they dismiss it with silence? Do they discuss it? What do they think the child's attitude is? We also ask whether the child has had any previous treatment for his stuttering.

Speech Behaviors

Next, we try to tape record five minutes of the client's speech while we talk about a number of topics. We also want to record at least five minutes of the client's oral reading. The clinician, interested in disfluency rather than reading ability, carefully selects a reading passage that is at or below the child's reading level. From these samples she determines stuttering frequencies, speaking rates, and severity levels of stuttering. These measures can be used in documenting changes during treatment and in preparing Individual Education Programs (IEP's).

Trial Therapy

In addition to the assessment of attitudes and stuttering severity, the clinician tries to find out how the child will respond to both stuttering modification and fluency shaping trial therapy.

In stuttering modification trial therapy, the clinician begins by assessing the effect of encouraging the child to stutter openly. The child is given a small reward for each stutter he has during reading or talking. (Pennies are excellent and inexpensive reinforcers for elementary school children.) After a few minutes of this procedure, many children will stutter markedly less or will stutter in a much easier fashion. The clinician then should praise and discuss the improvement and explore the child's ability to continue speaking more easily without tangible reward. If this procedure produces substantial changes in the child, a stuttering modification approach might be most effective for this child.

You will also want to assess the child's response to fluency shaping therapy. Since we will be talking later about using a structured hierarchy of fluency for treatment, we will describe how to find the basal fluency level with this approach. The stimuli for this trial therapy are 20 picture cards that can be easily identified by the child.

The clinician first models the name of each card, using a slow and relaxed speech pattern, after which the client says it in the same way. The clinician praises him if he says the word without stuttering, and this continues throughout the procedure. He is not praised if he stutters, but the clinician simply continues to the next item. If the child names most of the pictures without stuttering (for example, 18 out of 20)[1] the clinician moves to the next higher stage in the sequence: the child names the picture without a model. If he can name most of the 20 cards fluently, the clinician next has him say the name of the picture in a carrier phrase, such as, "This is a _____."
The child should say this spontaneously.

---

[1] These figures are based upon the observation that many fluency programs use criterion levels comparable to these. Thus, these guidelines will give the clinician some ideas as to where to begin her fluency shaping program.

In the last stage of the sequence, the child makes a spontaneous comment about each picture. If during any stage of this trial therapy the child stutters on many of his responses (for example, five or more) the clinician stops. If the clinician had to stop because the child experiences considerable stuttering, she should move to some play activity in which she models easy and relaxed speaking and the child gets the experience of fluency again. After a little of this, she may end the diagnostic session.

Comments on Selecting an Approach

The elementary school years are very important ones in the development of stuttering. Not only does overt speech behavior often become more severe, but feelings and attitudes about stuttering develop and become more handicapping. In reality, the six or seven year old is often more like the preschool stutterer. The twelve year old stutterer, on the other hand, can be more like the high school stutterer.

With these considerations in mind the authors feel that the stuttering modification approach and the fluency shaping approach begin to become more similar at the elementary school age level; this is particularly true for the lower age range of the group we are currently discussing. Thus, selecting the most appropriate approach for a given child becomes much more ambiguous. Our hunch is that the significant variable here is the child's feelings and attitudes about his speech, but at this point this hunch still isn't validated.

For many children in this group, especially those in the lower age range, our goal is spontaneous fluency. These children will often become normal speakers. For children in the upper age range of this group, especially those with maladaptive attitudes, the goal more realistically is controlled fluency or acceptable stuttering. Again, these positions aren't proven; they are only what our experience has suggested.

Indications for Stuttering Modification Therapy

Feelings and Attitudes

In the preceding chapter on high school and adult stutterers, we described some of the signs of avoidance conditioning that will suggest that a stuttering modification approach may be most appropriate. Here again, we look for indication of avoidance learning in speech behaviors and attitudes. Does the child show obvious signs of struggle on his face? Are most of his blocks frozen articulatory postures, rather than repetitions? Are there indications of severe laryngeal blocking, such as stoppage of phonation during stutters? Does the child usually have a hoarse vocal quality?

The clinician tries to find how the child feels about talking. Is he reluctant to talk? Does his A-19 score indicate that he doesn't like to talk in many situations? Does his body language suggest that he feels pretty bad about his speech? If the answers to many of these questions are "yes," then a speech modification approach is preferable.

Information from the parents is also helpful in making this choice. If they say the child is upset by or ashamed of his stuttering, or if they tell you by describing their reactions and the child's that he undergoes a lot of punishment for his stuttering, he would probably benefit from a stuttering modification approach.

Speech Behaviors

The frequency of the child's stuttering is not as important as his feelings about his speech. Many children in this age range have not yet developed negative feelings about their speech and will need little help for this aspect of stuttering. Others, however, are beginning to respond with fear and avoidance. They may exhibit word substitutions, circumlocutions, telegraphic speech and other attempts to avoid stuttering. They need therapy aimed at desensitizing them to stuttering.

Trial Therapy

The results of the trial therapy will help in planning treatment. If the child shows marked improvement in stuttering modification trial therapy, this approach may benefit him. Moreover, if in fluency shaping trial therapy, he is uncomfortable with the structured format, or if he stutters considerably before reaching the spontaneous sentence level, he may be better suited to stuttering modification than fluency shaping therapy.

In general, stuttering modification therapy is indicated for elementary school students when many of the following things are true: (1) they are very embarrassed or upset by stuttering, their home and school environment punishes it, (2) they respond well to stuttering modification trial therapy, or (3) they find it difficult to maintain fluency and interest in a fluency shaping trial therapy hierarchy.

Indications for Fluency Shaping Therapy

Attitudes and Feelings

In the initial evaluation of an elementary school stutterer, the clinician evaluates the child's reaction to his stuttering from his body language, facial expressions, and degree of talkativeness. Many children stutter frequently but with short blocks and little awareness of their stuttering.

A number of elementary school age stutterers don't notice their stuttering; in many it is a relatively minor nuisance. These children's parents are usually also not too upset by the child's stuttering. As a consequence, although they may tell him to "slow down" or "take your time," they would not be likely to punish him for it. If these things are true and the parents are willing to carry out a program of home management, the child is a good candidate for fluency shaping.

Speech Behavior

Again, frequency is not as important here as the child's reaction to his stuttering. When children exhibit rather neutral or mildly negative attitudes toward their stuttering, when they stutter openly and easily without avoidance behaviors, they would be good candidates for a fluency shaping program.

Trial Therapy

The child's progress in the fluency hierarchy is another good indicator of his readiness for fluency shaping. If he can go up the ladder to total fluency-at least on 15 or more of the 20 spontaneous sentences-he will probably succeed at the other steps in the program.

Indications for a Combined Approach

Elementary school age stutterers aren't usually clearly candidates for one approach or the other. When the emotional component is strongly present or when it is obviously absent, the decision is clear cut, but most children aren't like this. That is why we lean toward a combined approach. In a combined approach, potential feelings and attitudes are dealt with and an efficient procedure is used to establish fluent speech. Thus, our recommendation would be to use a combined approach unless conditions suggest otherwise.

Treatment Procedures

Stuttering Modification Therapy

The first aim of stuttering modification treatment for the elementary school age stutterer is to help him reduce the abnormality of his stuttering. This is usually done by helping him learn to react to his stuttering less emotionally. Most elementary school stutterers have learned to do the wrong things when speaking under stress: to tense, to struggle, to anticipate difficulty, and to avoid. Our job is to help the young stutterer respond differently. He needs to tackle a word he anticipates or experiences trouble on with a relaxed, but forward-moving approach.

We recommend the general progression outlined by Van Riper in his chapter on treating the young confirmed stutterer in The Treatment of Stuttering (Van Riper, 1973). If the child has mild or moderate stuttering, the modification of stuttering can begin at the same time as desensitization. As Van Riper suggests, the clinician's model of an easier type of stuttering can be very powerful in helping the child learn new behaviors. The clinician can model both the behavior of more relaxed stuttering and a calm attitude about getting stuck.

Through his interest and deep acceptance of the child and his speech, the clinician decreases the child's negative feelings about himself and his speech. Much of the treatment is done in games and activities in which the child can lose himself a little in the spirit of friendly competition. We devise games in which easier and easier stuttering is used. We try to arrange it so the child feels interested and excited about manipulating his stuttering and feels good about winning (which he does often). Below are some more details of treatment.

The clinician models a slow, relaxed direct form of stuttering. Since the elementary school child is likely to be aware of (and probably worried about) his stuttering, it is important to talk about the stuttering as well as model it. At first the clinician comments about her pseudo-stuttering when she does it, then she comments about the child's stuttering, with interest and acceptance. Hard ways of getting stuck are contrasted with easy ways. The child and the clinician play games where they try to catch each other stuttering or where they tell each other what kind of stutters to have. Rewards can be tokens or other desirable objects or activities.

Both fake stutters and real stutters are played with in their easy and hard versions. The major goal is to help the child develop a mild, easy, normal-sounding disfluency in place of a tense block or an avoidance. To reach this goal the child must become less afraid of his stuttering and more in touch with his mouth when he is about to say a word that used to trouble him.

The details of this course of treatment are well described by Van Riper in the chapter mentioned above. There are also excellent approaches to stuttering modification treatment by Dean Williams in Travis' *Handbook of Speech Pathology & Audiology* (Williams, 1971) and in sections of *Easy Talker* (Guitar & Reville, 1997). We have already called your attention to *Treating the School Age Child Who Stutters* (Dell, 2000) which is a detailed description of modeling.

It would probably be helpful for the clinician to tape record five minutes of conversation at the beginning of each session. This five minutes can give the clinician some idea of whether or not the child is getting the knack of making his stutters easier. If the stuttering isn't becoming easier by the third or fourth session, some change is needed.

It is also necessary to find out if change is taking place outside the treatment session, and to do this it is necessary to keep in touch with the child's parents and teachers. To foster transfer of easier speech into the child's natural environment, the clinician devises therapy programs that move in both "vertical" and "horizontal" directions. Vertical programming is a series of steps that teach the child something slightly nearer the final goal each time he masters another step.

In stuttering modification therapy, vertical programming is a matter of easier and easier ways of speaking. Horizontal programming, on the other hand, is generalizing a particular step. Here, it is helping the child use each step of easier speech in particular situations more and more like his normal environment. This can be done gradually by starting to practice a newly-mastered style of stuttering with one other child in the therapy room. Then the easier stuttering is done with two children, then with more children, then with the child's parents, with his teachers, and finally with any other people who may be cues for stuttering. Once this practice is done in the safe harbor of the treatment room, it can be gradually moved out into other situations.

We suggest starting with small steps and making larger ones if progress is going well. If generalization is difficult, it may mean that the child is still not desensitized and that fear of stuttering is disrupting his ability to stutter more easily. More time should be spent teaching the child to stay in touch with himself as he stutters. He can be taught to freeze his posture as he stutters and to feel comfortable with himself at that moment.

The tenser, more inappropriate stutters can be given plenty of negative practice in many situations until they lose their sting. On the other hand, problems in generalizing may also occur because the child simply hasn't had enough practice in the therapy room mastering a less struggled way of stuttering. If this is the reason generalization is difficult, the clinician goes back to easy stuttering activities.

Fluency Shaping Therapy

The goal of fluency shaping therapy for this age group is to establish fluency in a highly structured situation and gradually generalize it to the child's total daily speaking. A typical program would be Craig's program (Craig et al., 1996), Runyan and Runyan's program (Runyan and Runyan, 1999), Costello (1983), and Ryan's (2001) Gradual Increase in Length and Complexity of Utterance (GILCU) program. Ryan's program has three phases: establishment, transfer, and maintenance.

During the establishment phase, fluency is established in the presence of the clinician. In the transfer phase the fluency is transferred or generalized to daily speaking situations. Finally, in the maintenance phase the child's fluency is monitored over time. Measures of the child's stuttering are taken at the beginning, during and at the end of the program.

The establishment phase of the program might go as follows. The child begins by reading one word at a time fluently, then gradually increasing the length of his fluent reading up to five minutes. Some clinicians find it easier for the child if they model slow easy speech production for each step of the program. To go from one word to five minutes of fluent reading involves eighteen steps, e.g., one word, two words, three to six words, one to four sentences, etc. The child is reinforced for each fluent response, and there are criterion levels to tell the clinician when to move the child on to the next step.

After the child is able to read fluently for five minutes, he goes through another set of small steps to achieve fluency during five minutes of monologue and then five minutes of conversation. At this point the establishment phase has been completed.

Following the establishment phase is the transfer phase. Ryan will typically use a number of hierarchies or series of graded easy-to-hard activities to transfer the fluency from the clinical setting to the child's total speaking environment. The hierarchies would include: physical setting, audience size, and natural environment. By the use of these hierarchies, the clinician will help the child transfer his fluency to all situations he is likely to encounter.

In the maintenance phase of the program, the clinician gradually reduces her contact with the client. Periodic contacts are scheduled, however, and measurements of fluency are made.

Combined Approach

Many elementary school children are suited to a combined approach. Children who have a substantial amount of negative emotion, yet who tolerate structure well, may be excellent candidates for this blend of stuttering modification and fluency shaping approaches.

There are no studies of how to sequence stuttering modification and fluency shaping therapies most effectively. One alternative to the sequence described in the chapter on adult therapy (fluency shaping followed by stuttering modification) is to begin with stuttering modification treatment, then to use fluency shaping, first intensively and then with less frequency.

In this combined approach, stuttering modification therapy begins when the client confronts, explores and is desensitized to the stigma of stuttering and the moment of blockage. Our combined approach is given in a workbook for children entitled Easy Talker (Guitar & Reville, 1998). Also, the first sections of Van Riper's (1974) chapter on treating the young stutterer give excellent suggestions for these activities.

We have found that playing with the act of getting stuck is helpful in achieving desensitization. For example, fake stuttering in funny ways (done by both child and clinician) can take away some of the shame of being a stutterer. We also act out skits with puppets in which one character goes into wild gyrations of stuttering. Desensitization can also be achieved if the clinician and child go out onto the street and fake some stuttering to strangers and share their feelings afterwards. In this way, a little of the hostility and frustration of stuttering can be dissolved.

The chapter by Williams, mentioned above, describes another approach that is useful in diminishing a child's fear of stuttering. The clinician shows the child the similarity between making simple mistakes in everyday things and getting stuck in a stutter. By encouraging the attitude that stuttering is only another simple mistake, the clinician gradually teaches the child not to run away from his stutters, but to approach them less tensely and less fearfully. We recommend Van Riper's chapter for a fuller understanding of the philosophy behind his approach.

The activities in this chapter blend well with the fluency shaping activities that follow the initial stuttering modification procedures. The emphasis on what one is doing to interfere with smooth talking can help the stutterer after fluency shaping if he begins to interfere with the smooth fluency learned on DAF.

After five or six hours of stuttering modification therapy, the clinician should determine if the child's negative emotions toward his speech have diminished. The clinician's judgment and the A-19 Scale or the Communication Attitudes Test–Revised help in assessing this change. The severity of the stutterer's blocks should also have decreased. Once fear has been lowered substantially, fluency shaping begins. Intensive (five or six hours a day for two days) fluency shaping begins. Intensive fluency shaping gives a child extremely fluent spontaneous speech quickly, particularly if the child has been prepared for it with prior stuttering modification treatment.

The fluency shaping we advocate for the combined approach with this age group is DAF treatment. The procedures are the same as those for an adult. If a DAF machine is unavailable, the procedures suggested for the fluency shaping section of combined therapy for the high school and adult stutterer can be used. This involves modeling of slow prolonged speech.

Following transfer of fluency to the child's school and home situations, the clinician reintroduces fear-reducing stuttering modification procedures and continues fluency shaping techniques to help maintain fluency. Fake stuttering, open discussion of one's own stuttering, asking friends and family to help monitor speech rate and fluency may all be helpful for maintenance.

Case History

Ricky was a twelve-year-old boy who stuttered with repetitions, prolongations, and silent fixations. He showed laryngeal tension during stuttering, as well as respiratory discoordination. A modified version of the Erickson scale[1], couched in language appropriate for a twelve year old, showed a score of 17/24.

The clinician met with Ricky two to three times a week at the start. Treatment first focused on changing Ricky's attitudes toward his stuttering by helping him identify what he did when he stuttered. Videotapes and mirrors were used, and gradually Ricky became more objective about his stuttering. Then he learned to fake stutter, but this was done in a careful hierarchy to ensure that Ricky confronted his fears in successively greater doses. The modified Erickson scale now showed a score of six.

At this point the clinician prepared Ricky for intensive fluency shaping by practicing slow prolonged speech as in the combined treatment for the adult. After several bi-weekly sessions, treatment was intensified during two days of five and a half hours each. On these days, Ricky went through a DAF fluency shaping procedure in which he was reinforced for normal breath flow and prosody as well

---

[1] The Erickson was given because the A-19 Scale had not been devised at the time of this treatment.

as slow speech. As he passed each goal of the program (three minutes of fluency at progressively faster rates), Ricky was given tangible reinforcements or time off to play a variety of games.

After a day and a half, normal sounding fluency had been established and generalization began. Several of Ricky's classmates (chosen by him) were brought into the treatment room, one at a time, and Ricky spoke fluently for three minutes to each one. Then Ricky spoke to classmates outside the treatment room and to teachers in the hallway.

Finally, he made a phone call to a stranger. At this point Ricky was fluent in most situations.

Non-intensive therapy was resumed the following week and transfer activities continued. For two more months, until the end of school, Ricky went through as many different transfer situations as the clinician could think of. By the end of the year, his stuttering frequency was below one-percent syllables stuttered talking to a teacher. A year later he was again assessed and found to be at 1.6% SS.

During the intervening year, maintenance activities consisted of several meetings with Ricky to analyze remaining disfluencies, to fake stutter in old ways, and to reinforce his fluency. A further description of this program is available in the article by Turnbaugh and Guitar (1981).

Indications for Change in Approaches

As you will recall, when we discussed the high school and adult stutterer we suggested that there would be times when you would want to change approaches. This is true for elementary and junior high school stutterers, too.

Changing From a Stuttering Modification Approach

Sometimes a student at the upper age range of this group has trouble confronting his fear of stuttering. If the clinician has exhausted her stuttering modification techniques and has given as much support as possible, changing to fluency shaping or a combined approach may forestall the feelings of anger and frustration that accompanies repeated failure. The clinician explains to the child that everyone has trouble doing things they're afraid of and that there is another way he can be helped. The goal is to get fluency by some fluency shaping procedure. With increased fluency it is easier for the client to approach his fears since there is less to be afraid of. See the case of Ricky.

Changing From a Fluency Shaping Approach

The same problems we commented upon in the chapter on high school and adult stutterers apply here as well. Typical problems in fluency shaping are: 1) the client is unable to generalize his fluency because of residual speech fears, and 2) the stutterer has not developed an effective speech control to cope with the moment of stuttering when it occurs in the real world. The same suggestions given earlier are applicable here, too, as the clinician turns to a combined approach.

For the first problem, the client needs desensitization, and for the second he needs to learn some techniques to cope with feared words. The reader is referred to "Indications for Change in Approaches" in the chapter on the high school and adult stutterer.

Fluency Maintaining Strategies

As we indicated earlier in the section entitled "Comments on Selecting an Approach," the children in this group cover a wide age range, so it is realistic to have different goals. With younger elementary children it is reasonable to expect spontaneous fluency. For the children at the other end of the age range in this group, controlled fluency or acceptable stuttering are probably more realistic goals. These goals are the same regardless of the therapy approach that is used: stuttering modification, fluency shaping, or combined.

Many of the comments made under "Fluency Maintaining Strategies" for the high school and adult stutterer also apply here. This is particularly true for the older elementary school child. Some of these children are able to use control techniques, such as slow prolonged speech when their fluency is threatened after therapy. Most younger elementary school children, however, should probably not be expected to use controls or to implement conscious stuttering modification strategies to maintain fluency over the long haul after treatment. With these children the clinician must rely on spontaneous fluency developing, and luckily this often happens.

Chapter 5

the preschool child
who stutters

Diagnostic Procedures

Speech Behaviors

When an anxious mother calls and reports that her three year old son is "stuttering up a storm," the clinician will of course want to see the child and his parents as soon as possible. At first the clinician interviews the parents in a situation where the child can't hear the conversation. As the child plays in another room, the clinician finds out what speech behaviors the parents are concerned about. Many diagnostic signs help the clinician decide if the child is only normally disfluent or is really beginning to stutter.[1]

If the parents report that the child is occasionally repeating whole words and phrases, is not much concerned about them, and shows no signs of struggle or tension, the child is probably only normally disfluent. The parents should be told that their child is probably no more hesitant than most children his age. There are some activities, however, which these parents may wish to engage in to promote the growth of their child's fluency. These include speaking more slowly and simply to their child than they speak to adults, trying not to interrupt their child, and listening to

---

[1] The book *If Your Child Stutters: A Guide for Parents* (7th edition, 2008) and the DVD *Stuttering and The Preschool Child: Help for Parents* (2005) are excellent sources of information to help you decide if the child is beginning to stutter. They are listed in the references.

what the child is saying, rather than to the disfluencies. You may suggest they bring their child in again if his disfluencies worsen.

On the other hand, the child's parents may describe the disfluencies as being repetitions or prolongations of parts of words or monosyllabic words. The disfluencies may also show signs of struggle and tension. The clinician checks this out by talking with the child while engaging in a simple game or other activity.

A sample of speech can be recorded for careful listening later. If the child is entirely fluent, but the parents have described him as stuttering quite a bit, the sample may not be representative, and the clinician may want to put a little gentle pressure on the child's speech by asking a few questions. This often brings out disfluency, particularly if the question requires a long complicated answer. In this situation, we often ask how a familiar game such as Fish or Jacks is played.

In addition to the child's disfluencies, the clinician tries to assess the amount of fear the child has of speech or of stuttering. The child's willingness to talk, amount of eye contact, facial expression, and other body language give hints about feelings. The clinician also gauges how smooth the child's fluent speech is and how much he likes to talk, information that is useful in determining the approach to treatment.

A tape recording of the child's speech provides for a closer evaluation of the amount and type of disfluency. As with older stutterers, the frequency of the child's stuttering, and the speaking rate should be measured. One of the two previously mentioned severity scales should also be used. If recording the child's speech is impossible, at least count the number of disfluencies in a five minute period and note the things the child is actually doing when he is disfluent.

Feelings and Attitudes

The clinician also assesses in depth the feelings and attitudes of the parents toward their child's speech. This is important because the parents' feelings toward the stuttering will soon become the child's feelings. Do they worry that they have done something wrong in raising their child or are they only mildly concerned? Are they embarrassed by the stuttering? What is their response to a flurry of disfluencies? Do they tell their child to slow down or think before he speaks?

As the clinician explores the parents' feelings and their responses to the stuttering, she should praise the parents for helpful things that they may already be doing. These responses are fully elaborated in *If Your Child Stutters: A Guide for Parents* (7th edition, 2006). As the clinician talks to parents about these matters, she shares some of her knowledge about stuttering. This puts the parents at ease and smoothes the way for gathering information.

In addition to exploring the parents' attitudes about the child's speech, the clinician gets their impressions of the child's attitudes. How aware, how concerned, and how ashamed is the child about his stuttering? Parents can often tell if the child is embarrassed when stuck on a word, or just after. Many children even cry out with some verbal sign of frustration such as, "Mommy, why can't I talk?" Often, these are just passing moments and may not be remembered, but some children feel deeply the frustration and penalty of stuttering. These children need therapy activities that deal with their feelings about stuttering.

Trial Therapy

If the child shows repetitions or prolongations of syllables, and if the child is struggling, the clinician should do some trial therapy. This would be especially true if the clinician's observations of the child's speech coincided with the parents'.

In trial therapy the clinician wants to find out if the child can become fluent with some therapeutic approach, and how the child responds to a fluency hierarchy. The procedures used with elementary children outlined in the previous chapter under trial fluency shaping therapy may also be used with preschoolers.

If during any stage of this trial therapy the child stutters on many of his responses (for example, 5 or more out of 20) the clinician stops and notes if the child was bothered by the stuttering. If so, it is usually best to move to some play activity in which the clinician does a lot of easy and relaxed speaking and the child gets the experience of fluency again.

If the child is still stuttering, however, the clinician may want to try stuttering modification procedures. The clinician models easier versions of the child's stuttering. Using these models the clinician attempts to teach the child an easier form of stuttering. These modeling procedures are fully described in *Treating the School Age Child Who Stutters* (Dell, 2000).

The following section describes how to use diagnostic information to determine treatment. After the clinician has had time to consider her observations, she talks with the parents about her impressions of the child's speech. The section on treatment procedures offers specific suggestions of things the parents can do once treatment is determined.

Comments on Selecting an Approach

Preschool children who stutter have different feelings about their speech than adults and older children who stutter. Few preschoolers have the negative feelings that the older stutterer does. They may be aware of their stuttering and may even be frustrated by it; however, they are less likely to feel embarrassed, afraid, ashamed or guilty. This makes the clinician's job much easier.

The primary goal of treatment is increasing the child's fluency. Our goal is spontaneous fluency. Children generalize their fluency much more readily and permanently than older school students or adults who stutter, and rarely need controlled fluency. There are some children for whom attention will have to be given to feelings and attitudes, but even then not to the degree that is needed with the older stutterer.

We believe that stuttering modification and fluency shaping approaches are quite similar in the treatment of the preschool child. The goal of both approaches is to achieve a basal level of fluency and generalize that to other situations. The procedures of the two approaches for reaching this goal, however, may differ somewhat. Stuttering modification may, for example, model a slow and easy form of speaking for the child to emulate, whereas fluency shaping may begin with a short fluent response and increase its length and complexity.

Indications for Stuttering Modification Therapy

Speech Behaviors

Many of the behaviors of the preschool stutterer seem to result from avoidance learning. He may squeeze his lips or tense his vocal folds, causing his pitch to rise, to avoid the feeling of helplessness when syllables and sounds are repeated over and over and over again. He may avoid speech altogether and not say much at all if he fears disfluency when talking to a new person in a strange situation. He may hide his face or look embarrassed when stuck on a word or sound. These behaviors suggest that some attention should be given to the child's feelings.

Feelings and Attitudes

Therapy should be directed at reducing negative feelings if the child's parents say they are very uncomfortable when their child stutters. The same is true if they punish the child for stuttering, or if they say that the child is upset with the way he talks. Overall, the parents' as well as the child's attitudes and behaviors will suggest that disfluency is not tolerated.

Trial Therapy

The results of trial therapy will help the clinician to determine which approach is needed for the child. If the child has difficulty achieving fluency in the early stages of the fluency hierarchy, a stuttering modification approach is indicated. Clinical judgment is required to decide if the child will be frustrated by a fluency hierarchy in which he fails on several trials and is not rewarded for repeated tries.

The clinician also gauges how the child responds to the demands of structure itself. If a child is overactive or easily frustrated, it is another sign that stuttering modification therapy would be appropriate. Another indication for stuttering modification therapy would be a positive response to the stuttering modification trial therapy, i.e., the modeling of easier versions of the child's stuttering.

Indications for Fluency Shaping Therapy

Speech Behaviors

Most preschool children who stutter are excellent candidates for a fluency shaping approach to treatment. Fluency shaping is easy to implement and with the right child, it can be extremely efficient. A child who is a good candidate for this approach will show few signs of shame, guilt, or hostility. Instead of looking away or hiding his face when he stutters, the child will talk blithely on through blocks or repetitions, being not much deterred by his stuttering.

Feelings and Attitudes

These children's parents do not punish stuttering severely. Although they are unhappy that their child stutters, they are fairly tolerant of stuttering when it occurs.

In general, the child is well suited for a fluency shaping approach if his level of emotional response to stuttering is relatively low.

Trial Therapy

In addition to the child's response to the stuttering and his parents' attitudes, the ease with which he goes up the fluency hierarchy is an important consideration. Can he produce single words easily and fluently when they are modeled in slow and easy speech? Can he go up the ladder fairly well, at least to the stage of saying the word in a sentence?

The child's response to the structure itself is important. Can he easily tolerate sitting still and working hard for a half an hour? If this child does progress fairly well up the hierarchy and works well in structure, a fluency shaping approach is indicated.

Indications for a Combined Approach

Most of the children we have seen cannot be easily categorized as candidates for stuttering modification or for fluency shaping treatment. This is in line with our earlier comments that we see stuttering modification and fluency shaping therapy goals being similar for the preschool child. Many clinicians, moreover, even though comfortable with one of these two approaches, may want to try a new one. For these and other reasons, we suggest that you try a combined approach.

Treatment Procedures

Stuttering Modification

The basic aim in this approach is to modify the preschool child's stuttering so it is more like normal disfluency. Normal disfluencies are slow and easy repetitions of whole words and syllables. They terminate with a relaxed sound, rather than an abrupt ending. Normal disfluencies may also be slight prolongations of initial sounds but they sound relaxed. Gradually the child outgrows these disfluencies if they remain loose, slow, and easy, as the child's speech matures.

If the child is not too aware of his disfluency, therapy follows an approach similar to an integrated treatment for the borderline stutterer in *Stuttering: An Integrated Approach to Its Nature and Treatment* (Guitar, 1998). The clinician models easy disfluencies, and the child's parents are encouraged to do this also.

Since the heart of this approach is to model for the child what he should sound like, it is worthwhile to practice these easy disfluencies. Listen to them on a tape recorder. Make sure they have the following qualities:

1. Only one or two repetitions of a word or syllable are used. Like-like this, rather than like-like-like-like this.

2. Between repeated words or syllables airflow or voicing should be continuous, loose, and easy, not broken, tight, or tense.

3. When the clinician models slight prolongations, her voice is very relaxed, and she makes a smooth transition from the first sound into the rest of the word. L-l-like this, without tightening any part of the speech mechanism.

4. Disfluencies should be slow; in fact, most of the model's speech with the child should be slow.

5. The clinician shouldn't overdo disfluencies. It is a good idea to listen to how frequently the child stutters and model disfluencies at about that frequency or less.

Modeling can be done by the clinician as she and the child play together with toys. Rather than go into much detail about modeling disfluencies, we refer you to the excellent book, *Treating The School-Age Child Who Stutters: A Guide for Clinicians*, by Dell (2000).

Since the aim of modeling is to diminish the severity of disfluency, the clinician must keep track of the child's reactions. Perhaps the best way to do this is to tape record most sessions and continually assess the frequency and severity of disfluencies. If the child originally had hard blocks, are they easing off into looser ones? If the child had many tense repetitions of syllables, is the number of repetitions on a syllable diminishing and do the repetitions sound more relaxed?

If, after three or more sessions, the clinician detects no change in the child's stuttering, she should think about dealing more directly with the child's attitude. Remember, the stuttering modification approach is used with a child who appears to be reacting negatively to his disfluency, so the clinician should be working on helping the child feel more comfortable when he encounters difficulty with his fluency.

If modeling alone isn't changing the stuttering, the clinician begins to talk about stuttering with the child, commenting on her own modeled disfluencies. She may engage the child in puppet play where the puppets talk about getting stuck (or whatever phrase seems appropriate to describe the child's stuttering). She may play games where she and the child have fun catching each other's stutterings, pretending to stutter, or comparing hard and easy ways of getting stuck.

If possible, one or both parents should be involved in the sessions. Once the clinician and child are comfortable with each other, one parent can participate in part of a session. Usually the parent won't feel comfortable at first, pretending to stutter, but with encouragement, he or she will join in more and more. A part of each session is spent talking to the parents about their observations and feelings about the child's progress. As the parents become more involved in treatment, their attitudes about disfluency will probably change. They will most likely become facilitators of long term fluency.

If it is not feasible to involve the parents in treatment, the clinician should still try to talk to them, in person or on the phone, about the goals of treatment and about their feelings about the child's speech. If they are particularly unreceptive, they may also be unaccepting of their child's disfluency. In this case, efforts to desensitize the child to pressures on his speech may be particularly needed.

Once the child has developed fluency or easy disfluency, the clinician begins to introduce a little pressure on the child's speech. The purpose of this kind of treatment is to help the child build up some resistance to fluency disruptors. Usually disruption is introduced in a playful way. The clinician explains that the game is taking turns trying to make the other one stutter, begins by asking the child to pound on the table or make faces while the clinician describes a picture. The clinician fakes a slight breakdown in fluency, comments on it, and says the word again with an easier disfluency. Then it is the child's turn.

It is important that the clinician's first attempts at disrupting the child are interpreted by the child as fun. She may make faces or sing. Desensitization should chase away some of the shame and solemnity of stuttering. The child should succeed at retaining fluency many times before he fails, and the clinician should have plenty of failures before the child fails.

By using stresses and pressures more and more like those in the child's environment and pressing the child to greater and greater resistance, the clinician makes therapy a real confidence-boosting experience and paves the way for long-term fluency.

Greater detail on this and other stuttering modification strategies are available in *The Treatment of Stuttering* by Van Riper (1973), in *Stuttering: An Integrated Approach to Its Nature and Treatment* (Guitar, 2006) and in *Stuttering and Related Disorders of Fluency* (Conture & Curlee, 2007).

Fluency Shaping Therapy

The goal of this approach is simply to teach the child to talk fluently with the clinician, and then gradually transfer that fluency to all other situations. This approach is similar to the Gradual Increase and Complexity of Utterance (GILCU) program described in the earlier chapter on elementary school children who stutter. There is one difference, however, with this program for preschoolers. With school age children the GILCU program included portions involving reading and monologue. These would most likely be inappropriate for the preschooler.

We will not discuss a GILCU program for preschoolers in depth at this point. The reader can get a flavor for one from reading the description of a GILCU program in the earlier chapter and from reading the following section on a combined approach. In that section an approach is presented within a GILCU structure. Recent fluency-shaping approaches to this age group can be found in *Stuttering and Related Disorders of Fluency* (Conture & Curlee, 2007).

We also recommend the Lidcombe program for preschool children (Onslow, Packman & Harrison, 2003). This is a parent-administered approach that requires some specialized training for the clinician. Information on training workshops in North America can be found at www.montrealfluency.com.

Combined Approach

Earlier we described a fluency hierarchy that tested the child's ability to speak fluently in a series of graded tasks. The same hierarchy can be used as the beginning of treatment for the preschool stutterer. We will review that hierarchy here.

The reader may also wish to turn back to the section on a fluency hierarchy in diagnosis. The fluency hierarchy consists of six goals, as follows:

Goal 1: Fluent Response, Single Word, Modeling. The clinician begins by modeling a slow, fluent response. The first sub-goal is finding the degree of slowness and easiness to model in order to have the child be fluent when he names each picture. We also recommend that the clinician use slow, easy speech when talking during the therapy session. In this stage of fluency shaping, as in later stages, the clinician should be careful to reward the child for success and ignore failure. When he says the word fluently, the clinician says something like, "That was good; that was good easy talking." If the child feels that the clinician is genuinely interested in him and fun to play with, her praise will be a strong reward. A token economy can also be used in the beginning. This way the child earns some small tangible reward when he has accumulated sufficient tokens or when a goal has been achieved.

We suggest a pre-set criterion of success for the child to achieve at each level before progressing to the next level. This criterion should assure that the child is fluent most of the time. The criterion should also allow a little leeway so the child isn't frustrated when he stutters just once or twice and must repeat the level. Clinical judgment helps in deciding whether to set the level for passing at 18 or 19 fluent utterances, for example, out of 20 utterances.

Goal 2: Fluent Response, Single Word, Without Modeling. After going through the cards with modeling, the clinician then goes through the same cards without the modeling. At this stage the purpose is to make sure the child can produce the fluent response without prompting. The clinician keeps working at this stage until satisfied that the child can produce single word responses fluently without requiring a model of the word he says.

Goal 3: Fluent Response, Phrase, Without Modeling. At the beginning of this stage the clinician chooses a simple phrase such as, "That's a _____ " that can be used with the names of more pictures. The child goes through the cards again, using the carrier phrase, and inserting the name of the picture in easy, fluent speech. Before leaving this stage, the child should be able to produce the entire phrase, including the picture name, without stuttering.

To reach this sub-goal, cards for stuttered words may have to be set aside temporarily. Then, when other words are said fluently, the client can return to the stuttered ones and work on them. The clinician must first model them slowly.

Finally, with adequate practice of slow fluency, the child will be able to go through pictures previously stuttered. The clinician works quickly and with enthusiasm to keep the child's interest up and his frustration level down. The token economy will also help the child's motivation.

Goal 4: Fluent Response, Sentence, Without Modeling. In this phase the clinician shows the child a picture and has him say something about it. He can comment about what is happening in the picture, what color it is, if he likes the object, etc. The clinician continues to use slow easy fluency when talking to the child, and she also continues verbally and tangibly reinforcing the child for fluent utterances. When the child is fluent at this level he goes on to the next.

Goal 5: Fluent Response, Spontaneous Conversation. In this long phase the child reaches fluency in conversational speech in the treatment setting. The phase begins with games such as "Giant Steps," in which short specific responses are required, or puppet play in which short responses are typical. Gradually opportunities for longer and longer responses are introduced, until all of the child's speech in the treatment setting is fluent.

Rewards are given for success and failures are ignored. The clinician also gives clear instructions to the child that he needs to use the special slow and easy speech that he has been practicing. Daily records of the child's level of disfluency are kept. When he is fluent at this level the next phase begins.

Goal 6: Fluent Response, Spontaneous Speech, Outside of Treatment Room. When the child has been essentially fluent for an entire session it is time to transfer fluency outside. Many young stutterers will transfer fluency spontaneously, but to be on the safe side, it is a good idea to select some crucial situations and carry out transfer therapy in them.

If the child is being treated in a school or clinic, the most important transfer situation is the child's home. The child's mother or father, or both, come to treatment and the clinician first makes sure that the child is fluent with them in an easy play situation. It may be necessary to slow everyone's speech rate to ensure this. Once the child is fluent in this situation, the clinician, conferring with the parents, selects a typical situation at home that has produced little stuttering for the child. Then that situation is role-played with plenty of enthusiasm and reinforcement, the child's fluency being maintained via whatever technique has worked before. The next step is to have the parent play the same situation with the child a few times at home with plenty of fluency support.

Next, the clinician selects, with the parents, a situation that has been a little more difficult for the child at home, and has the parents go through this situation with him, reinforcing him for "good easy talking." In this way the parents will gradually generalize the child's fluency to all situations. We find that there is considerable spontaneous generalization of fluency occurring at this time, too.

The clinician continues to select difficult situations, role-playing them in the treatment setting and then at home until all potential trouble spots are taken care of. Because stuttering appears to vary with physical well-being and emotional well-being, it is not unusual to see some backward slippage in the child's fluency. If the child can be taught to respond to suddenly difficult situations by slowing down and talking easily, his resistance to relapse will be stronger.

Case History

Doug was a four-year-old boy who had been stuttering for about six months, according to his parents. He stuttered on approximately six percent of his spoken words. He was aware of his stuttering. A few times his friends in the neighborhood had teased him about his speech. Doug did not exhibit many word or situation avoidances, but he did use different ways of speaking to be fluent. For example, he had learned that if he spoke in a high pitched voice, he could be fluent, and from time to time he would do this. During the initial evaluation, he responded very well to trial therapy. He was fluent at the word, phrase and sentence levels.

Therapy for Doug began at the one word level. The clinician modeled slow, easy talking for him and asked him to imitate her. He did this without any difficulty. The clinician verbally reinforced him ("good easy talking") after each fluent response. When asked what he wanted to earn in speech class, he said he wanted a hermit crab. Doug's mother agreed to buy him a hermit crab when he had earned enough tokens. A price was determined by the clinician.

After completing the one word level modeled by the clinician, Doug rapidly passed the level at which one word was to be said spontaneously. He then went on to complete the carrier phrase and sentence level without any difficulty. The conversational level also went well. Doug was a talkative child, and he and his clinician talked about many things. At about this point he earned his hermit crab because he had accumulated enough tokens. It was then agreed that Doug would work for a second hermit crab (Doug figured he would have baby crabs), and a price was set.

The next step was to transfer his fluency outside the therapy situation, specifically, to Doug's home. At this point Doug's mother was brought into therapy and she, Doug, and the clinician interacted until it was determined that Doug was fluent in this situation. Doug's mother also learned how to count stuttering behaviors and intermittently reinforce him for fluency.

Next, the clinician withdrew from the room and let Doug and his mother talk by themselves. When it was determined that Doug could be fluent talking to his mother alone, the clinician suggested that they do the same type activities at home. This went well. Mother reported that not only was Doug fluent with her at home in most situations, but that his fluency had generalized to the father and his friends. Doug seemed to have more difficulty talking with his older brother; therefore, the clinician brought the brother into the clinic to repeat the same steps used with Doug's mother.

There is one aspect of this program that should be commented upon. Doug was socially reinforced for saying things "easy." When he stuttered on a word, he didn't get any social or tangible reinforcer. Doug asked one day early in the program why he hadn't received a token. The clinician told him it was because he had said the word "hard." From that point on Doug and his clinician would often comment upon saying words "easy" or "hard."

Within this very structured and objective program, Doug began to talk about his speech very objectively. He knew when he spoke "easy" and he knew when he spoke "hard." He approached the whole thing in a very objective manner. There was no embarrassment or uneasiness on his part, and he talked about his speech objectively.

For example, one day the clinician saw Doug and his mother in a store, and Doug ran up to the clinician and began to talk with her. During this conversation, he had a small block. Doug responded by saying, "Oops, I said that hard." He then said it over "easy." Not only has Doug learned to be a great deal more fluent, he has also developed an objective attitude about his speech.

Indications for Change in Approaches

In the section, "Comments on Selecting an Approach" for preschool children, we said that the goals of the stuttering modification and the fluency shaping approaches become similar in treatment of the preschool stutterer. The thrust behind each approach is to facilitate the child's attaining greater fluency. Both approaches use various techniques to facilitate fluency in the child. For example, they may use modeling of easy stuttering or they may use modeling of slow, easy talking, or they may gradually expand the fluency from one word to a whole conversation.

The specific techniques may vary, but the goal is the same. Consequently, a change from one approach to another would merely be a change from one technique to another; it would not be a change in goals. For this reason, we see little need to change from one approach to the other in working with the preschool stutterer.

Fluency Maintaining Strategies

Earlier in this chapter we indicated that our goal for preschool children is spontaneous fluency. We also suggested that many, if not most, preschoolers generalize their fluency much more easily than do older stutterers. There is no need to teach these children to control their speech. Nor is there any need to teach them stuttering modification strategies. The clinician has to provide the setting in which the young stutterer can be fluent, and then provide the conditions that will allow this fluency to generalize. From there on Mother Nature will do the rest.

Epilogue

In writing this book, we were guided by several underlying assumptions. First, both authors believe from their own clinical experience that stutterers can be treated by stuttering modification, fluency shaping, or combined approaches, but this and other assumptions made are not firmly based on data.

Second, we believe that a successful fluency shaping program can lead to the deconditioning of word and situation fears. We realize that fear deconditioning is not the intended goal of fluency shaping, but we suspect that this is, in part, what really happens. We suspect that whereas fluency shaping can decondition many fears effectively and efficiently, what it cannot do that stuttering modification treatment may do is to decondition the fear of stuttering itself. Again, we have no data to substantiate this.

While we await data to support or refute it, the hypothesis may be useful as a guide for selecting treatment. If the clinician judges that the stutterer has much fear of stuttering, stuttering modification treatment may be needed; otherwise, fluency shaping may be more effective.

One of the authors has written an expanded version of this book entitled *The Nature and Treatment of Stuttering: An Integrated Approach,* 3rd Edition, should you want to read more. It is published by Lippincott, Williams, & Wilkins (1-800-638-3030, www.lww.com).

Third, the authors feel that the stutterer's feelings and attitudes about his speech are important and should be considered in the treatment of stuttering and in the assessment of treatment success. We realize that we talked glibly about feelings and attitudes in this book, but we are aware that there are many pitfalls involved in assessing them. We know it is not as simple as we made it sound.

Fourth, we both believe that it is important to gather and report data. We realize there are many problems in measuring change in stuttering therapy, but it needs to be done. Only when both stuttering modification and fluency shaping advocates do more data gathering will we begin to resolve the conflicts between the proponents of these two schools of stuttering treatment. It may well be up to the foot soldiers and not the generals to resolve these conflicts. It is, after all, the clinicians out in the field, out on the firing line, who care more deeply for their clients than for their theories. We hope it is they who will develop the true integration of treatments of stuttering.

References

Ainsworth, S., & Fraser, J. (2008). *If your child stutters: A guide for parents* (7th ed.). Memphis: Stuttering Foundation of America.

Andrews, G., & Cutler, J. (1974). Stuttering therapy: The relation between changes in symptom level and attitudes. *Journal of Speech and Hearing Disorders,* 39, 312-319.

Brutten, G. J., & Dunham, S. (1989). The Communication Attitude Test: A normative study of grade school children. *Journal of Fluency Disorders,* 14, 371-377.

Conditioning in stuttering therapy. (1970). Memphis: Stuttering Foundation of America.

Conture, E. G. (2001). *Stuttering: Its nature, diagnosis and treatment.* Boston: Allyn & Bacon.

Costello, J. M. (1983). Current behavioral treatment for children. In D. Prins & R. J. Ingham (Eds.), *Treatment of stuttering in early childhood: Methods and issues.* San Diego: College-Hill Press.

Conture, E. G. and Curlee, R. F. (2007). *Stuttering and related disorders of fluency* (3rd ed.). New York: Thieme.

Curlee, R. F., & Siegel, G. M. (1997). *Nature and treatment of stuttering: New directions* (2nd ed.). Boston: Allyn & Bacon.

Darley, F. L., & Spriestersbach, D. C. (1978). *Diagnostic methods in speech pathology.* New York: Harper & Row.

Dell, C. (2000). *Treating the school age child who stutters: A guide for clinicians* (2nd edition). Memphis: Stuttering Foundation of America.

Erickson, R. L. (1969). Assessing communication attitudes among stutterers. *Journal of Speech and Hearing Research,* 12, 711-724.

Gregory, H. H. (1979). *Controversies about stuttering therapy.* Baltimore: University Park Press.

Guitar, B. (1976). Pretreatment factors associated with the outcome of stuttering therapy. *Journal of Speech and Hearing Research,* 19, 590-600.

Guitar, B. (2006). *Stuttering: An integrated approach to its nature and treatment.* Baltimore: Lippincott, Williams & Wilkins.

Guitar, B., & Grims, S. (1977, November). *Developing a scale to assess communication attitudes in children who stutter.* Poster session presented at the annual meeting of the American Speech-Language-Hearing Association, Atlanta, GA.

Guitar, B., & Reville, J. (1998). *Easy talker.* San Antonio: Pro-Ed.

Hanna, R. & Owen, N. (1977). Facilitating transfer and maintenance of fluency in stuttering therapy. *Journal of Speech and Hearing Disorders, 42,* 65-76.

Helliesen, G. (2006). *Speech Therapy for the Severe Older Adolescent and Adult Stutterer: A Program for Change.* Newport News, VA.: Apollo Press. Available from www.apollopress.com

If you stutter: Advice for adults (2007). [DVD]. Memphis: Stuttering Foundation of America.

Luper, H. L., & Mulder, R. L. (1964). *Stuttering: Therapy for children.* Englewood Cliffs, NJ: Prentice-Hall.

Manning, W. H. (2001). *Clinical decision making in fluency disorders* (2nd ed.). San Diego: Singular Thompson Learning.

O'Brian, S., Onslow, M., Cream, A. & Packman, A. (2003) Camperdown Program: Outcomes of a new prolonged-speech treatment model. *Journal of Speech, Language, and Hearing Research, 46,* 933-946.

Onslow, M., Packman, A. & Harrison, E. (2002). *The Lidcombe Program of early stuttering intervention: A clinician's guide.* Austin, TX: Pro-Ed.

Perkins, W. (1973). Replacement of stuttering with normal speech. II. Clinical procedures. *Journal of Speech and Hearing Disorders, 38,* 295-303.

Riley, G. D. (1972). A stuttering severity instrument for children and adults. *Journal of Speech and Hearing Disorders, 37,* 314-322.

Riley, G. D. (1994). *Stuttering severity instrument for children and adults* (3rd ed.). Austin, TX: Pro-Ed.

Runyan, C., & Runyan, S. (1999). Therapy for school-age stutterers: An update of the Fluency Rules program. In R. Curlee (Ed.) *Stuttering and related disorders of fluency* (2nd ed.). New York: Thieme.

Rustin, L., Cook, F. & Spense, R. (1999). *The management of stuttering in adolescence: A communication skills approach.* London: Whurr.

Ryan, B. P. (2001). *Programmed therapy for stuttering in children and adults* (2nd ed.). Springfield, IL: C .C. Thomas.

Shapiro, D. A. (1999). *Stuttering intervention: A collaborative journey to fluency freedom.* Austin, TX: Pro-Ed.

Sheehan, J. G. (Ed.). (1970). *Stuttering: Research and therapy.* New York: Harper & Row.

Starbuck, H. (1974). *Videotapes on stuttering* [videotapes]. (Available from Stuttering Foundation of America, P.O. Box 11749, Memphis, TN 38111-0749).

Stuttering and its treatment (1961). Memphis: Stuttering Foundation of America.

Stuttering and the Preschool Child: Help for Parents (2005) [DVD]. Memphis: Stuttering Foundation of America.

Stuttering and your child: A video for parents (1996) [videotape]. Memphis: Stuttering Foundation of America.

Therapy in action: The school-age child who stutters (2005) [DVD]. Memphis: Stuttering Foundation of America.

Therapy for stutterers (1974). Memphis: Stuttering Foundation of America.

Turnbaugh, K., & Guitar, B. (1981). Short-term intensive stuttering treatment in a public school setting: An account. *Language, Speech and Hearing Services in the Schools,* 12, 107-114.

Van Riper, C. (1973). *The treatment of stuttering.* Englewood Cliffs, NJ: Prentice-Hall.

Van Riper, C. (1974). *Therapy in action* [DVD]. (Available from Stuttering Foundation of America, P.O. Box 11749, Memphis, TN 38111-0749).

Webster, R. L. (1974). A behavioral analysis of stuttering treatment and theory. In K. Calhoun et al (Eds), *Innovative treatment methods in psychopathology.* New York: John Wiley & Sons.

Williams, D. E. (1971). Stuttering therapy for children. In L. E. Travis (Ed.), *Handbook of speech pathology.* New York: Appleton-Century-Crofts.

Stuttering:

Basic Clinical Skills

More than three years in the making, this exciting new 2+ hour DVD demonstrates speech management strategies to help you work effectively with children and adults who stutter.

Dynamic demonstration of stuttering therapy techniques by experts from around the world:

- **Frances Cook,** MSc, Cert. CT (Oxford), Reg UKCP (PCT), Cert MRCSLT (Hons)
- **Willie Botterill,** MSc (Psych. Couns.), Reg UKCP (PCT), Cert MRCSLT
- **Ali Biggart,** MSc, BA (Hons), Dip. CT (Oxford), Cert MRCSLT
- **Alison Nicholas,** MSc, BA (Hons), Cert MRCSLT
- **Jane Bligh,** BSc (Hons), Cert MRCSLT
    From Michael Palin Centre for Stammering Children, London

• • • •

- **Barry Guitar,** Ph.D., University of Vermont
- **Peter Ramig,** Ph.D., University of Colorado-Boulder
- **Patricia Zebrowski,** Ph.D., University of Iowa
- **June Campbell,** M.A., private practice, Carmel, CA, provided additional footage.

If you believe this book has helped you or you wish to help this worthwhile cause, please send a donation to:

THE
STUTTERING
FOUNDATION®

A *Nonprofit Organization*
Since 1947—Helping Those Who Stutter

3100 Walnut Grove Road, Suite 603
P.O. Box 11749 • Memphis, TN 38111-0749
1-800-992-9392   901-452-7343
www.stutteringhelp.org
www.tartamudez.org